# ANDREW FLINTOFF

## SECOND INNINGS

### *My Sporting Life*

As told to Ed Smith

HODDER

First published in Great Britain in 2015 by Hodder & Stoughton
An Hachette UK company

First published in paperback in 2016

1

A CIP catalogue record for this title is available from the British Library

Paperback ISBN: 978 1 473 61659 2
Ebook ISBN: 978 1 473 61656 1

Typeset in Charter by Palimpsest Book Production Limited,
Falkirk, Stirlingshire

Printed and bound by Clays Ltd, St Ives plc

Hodder & Stoughton policy is to use papers that are natural, renewable
and recyclable products and made from wood grown in sustainable
forests. The logging and manufacturing processes are expected to
conform to the environmental regulations of the country of origin.

Hodder & Stoughton Ltd
Carmelite House
50 Victoria Embankment
London EC4Y 0DZ

www.hodder.co.uk

This book is dedicated to three people, none, sadly, still with us:

My amazing Nan

Jim Kenyon, my coach

Pete Marron, Lancashire legend and my first landlord

# CONTENTS

# 1

# TWO PEOPLE

THERE have always been two people jostling for control of my life, two totally opposite characters. The first one is super-confident, bulletproof, a showman and an extrovert. He tries to make people laugh, messes about, gets into trouble, shrugs it off. Then he jumps in at the deep end again, wondering if he'll be able to swim to safety.

The other character is withdrawn and reflective. He is certainly more complex and uncertain, often unsure why he puts himself into such weird and demanding situations.

Trouble is: they're both me.

There's 'Fred', the man who everyone knows, or at least they think they know him. Fred is the all-rounder who charged in and whacked a few sixes. It is Fred who fell off a pedalo after a night out in the Caribbean and got banned from the England team. It is Fred who became a professional boxer. It is Fred who has always found it hard to say no – to a new challenge, to another drink, to pushing the limits, to finding out how far he can go.

Then there is Andrew. The kid who never quite fitted in. At school he was picked on because he played cricket – a bit cissy, cricket, when you're growing up in a rough corner of Preston. Andrew has always been on the outside of groups, wondering how he is perceived, what people think of him. He is an introvert who dislikes competitiveness – especially his own. He hates hearing anyone tell him he's great at anything. There are long spells when the world's praise and prizes mean nothing to him – less than nothing, actually. He just wishes no one was looking at him. Some people would find Andrew pretty boring. Fred certainly would!

For a while, Fred really took over. But it got tiring – the pretence, the hard-man act, the whole extrovert persona. I guess the mask became the man. It was exhausting being that person. It was like being in a soap opera and gradually turning into the character you're acting. A lot of sportsmen are actors in a way. But it's a strange kind of acting. Because everyone knows that Rita from *Coronation Street* doesn't really work in that shop; she's got a proper name and a real job. But with sportsmen it's more complicated, and the lines between what's real and what's not get blurred.

I very rarely watch recordings of things from my past, whether it's playing cricket or fooling around on a TV programme. It's too uncomfortable. But a couple of years ago I was in a hospitality box and there was a video playing of the 2009 Ashes Test at Lord's. It was like watching somebody else bowling. At no stage did I think, 'That's me.' I felt no emotional attachment to the man on the screen, nothing.

I always had a connection with fans. I think a lot of them identified with me the cricketer, especially when I was doing well, because that's the person they wanted to be – not taking it too seriously but pulling it off on the day. That's the person I wanted to be, too. But in reality, I was just like the man in the stands who has his problems and his worries and insecurities. Fred on the outside, Andrew on the inside. Underneath it all, I'm much closer to the normal fan than I was to my own persona.

Life is more balanced now. I don't feel I have to put up those defences, to put on such a big show. And because I'm more confident inside, I don't feel the need to act so confident in public all the time. I can actually do what I want to do, not what I'm expected to want to do. I don't drink; I'm happy living day by day and taking life as it comes.

But I also know, if I'm really honest, that there will always be Fred. He's part of me, he's there. There is something inside me that is never satisfied – that's the nature of a performer. It's also true that though Fred got me into a lot of trouble, he also got me where I am today. And I won't lie: I've had a lot of fun.

So I guess this is the story of one life but two people. I'll be just as upfront about the lows as the highs. Here's the really strange thing: I don't find it hard to be totally honest, to let down my guard, to own up to massive mistakes. I'll tell you why. Because however critical some people might be, they'll never be as critical as I am of myself.

In professional sport everyone says you've got to find this balance, a happy medium – don't get too high, and never allow yourself to get too down. Emotional management – I think that's the trendy psychobabble phrase for it. Well, I could never find it, that elusive balance. I just couldn't. As a cricketer, I was always all over the place. Even as a kid, I'd be brilliant for a spell, then absolutely rubbish.

In some ways, I'm glad I didn't find that happy medium. Because it would have been dull. I was always at my best after I'd hit rock bottom. And I hit rock bottom plenty of times as a cricketer.

Looking back, though I never knew it at the time, subconsciously I must have engineered some of those crises, like I wanted to find the very bottom of the scale. Like I wanted to walk along the edge. Perhaps it's because I struggled with discipline in a conventional sense of the word. If, to my mind, something doesn't matter much either way, if I can't see the point, then often I can't be bothered to do what I ought to do.

But if I haven't got a choice, if I absolutely have to pull something out of the fire, then life feels simple again, my mind becomes clear.

I know I've always pushed my luck. But there is a strange kind of logic to the chances I've taken. I've always enjoyed the rebuilding phase, working my way back from being as low as I could sink. I've thrived on people writing me off. Because if you write me off, I'll shut you up.

As a cricketer, I played on bravado and character. My personality was bound up with how I played the game. When I bowled I tried to play on my size a bit and on the fact that I apparently never got tired, even though I usually was. Even when I batted, taking on the hook shot when there were two men back for the hook – yes, that was all bravado too. I wanted to project this carefree persona, to give the impression that I didn't care. All very Fred.

The reality was different. I was a secret trainer. Until my knees went, I used to do hill running up in Bolton, totally away from the team environment. But I never told anybody. I guess I was the opposite of a teacher's pet. I wanted everyone to think I was more of a maverick than I actually was.

And that includes my own mates. I wanted them to think I was different as well. I'd get changed at the last minute before it was my turn to bat. At Lord's, rather than watching play, I'd sit out the back and have a cigarette when I was next in. At the close of play I'd smoke in the ice bath as a way of measuring time. When I'd finished my fag, it was time to get out. (I can pull hard on a fag when I need to.)

I was bluffing myself as well as other people. It was all part of moving from one personality to the other. I'd have my breakfast in the team hotel with my wife and family. Then I'd kiss my daughter Holly goodbye, walk out of the hotel and start being Fred.

Fred, Andrew, Fred, Andrew.

It was tiring and it took its toll. But there may have been some method to the madness.

## 2

# THE BILLY ELLIOT OF CRICKET

M y young life was a bit like Billy Elliot's, only I didn't dance, I played cricket. I certainly wasn't destined to be a cricketer. The odds were stacked against.

We lived on the edge of four tough council estates. The two schools I went to were on those estates. I never played cricket at school. It was football all year round – football is easy, you just put two jumpers out as goals and get on with it.

Cricket was seen as the posh sport, and it was something that pushed me to the outside of groups. It was a health risk, being known to play cricket. Just getting through the day at school with my teeth intact was a challenge.

I think that's why sledging was usually wasted on me. Say what you like, Shane Warne, or whoever. Chirp up about my batting technique or my character. You're wasting your time. It's not going to make any difference. I'd been in so many situations that were a lot more threatening than listening to some nonsense on a nice cricket pitch. If you knew what I'd been through to get on to this field, you wouldn't bother with the verbals.

Outside school, cricket toughened me up quickly in other ways. My dad was captain of the second team at the local club. My older brother Chris and I were pushed around the boundary as babies. I played in an Under-14s match when I was six. No cricket whites back then, just a Manchester United tracksuit from the family across the road. It wasn't long before I was playing cricket against men.

The downside was a sense of apartness. I never really felt I belonged. At school I was the cricketer. Among cricketers, I was the only child in the room. I was always unsure what people thought of me, what people would say about me when I wasn't around. That bothered me for a long time.

At school, there was no cricket, but there was chess. I still love chess. Mr Minter ran the school chess club and you'd be surprised by the kids who turned up to play. We had all sorts in there, the least likely chess players ever.

But we had one of the best chess teams in the country. The hardest one, too.

I played chess for Lancashire, my brother played for England. At the age of eleven, there was already a glimpse of something in me, a will to win. Once, in a match against Staffordshire, I was playing this poor kid and I noticed that after a move he didn't press his clock as he was supposed to. The done thing would have been for me to say, 'Mate, you haven't pressed your clock.' But I was so keen to win that I just sat there for forty-five minutes scratching my head, pretending it was my move. Then his little flag dropped. Time up. He'd lost. So I stuck my hand out to thank him for the game, at which point he broke down into hysterical crying. I was hauled up before the chess federation for my ungentlemanly behaviour.

Competitiveness can bring out the best and the worst in me. Still does today. I sometimes play chess against my brother, but that ends up being frustrating because I can never beat him. I taught my boy Corey and we play together. I find it hard to let him win. I do every now and then. But I think you have to earn things. Victory has to mean something.

* * *

My mum worked at a school, doing lots of different things. Sometimes I'd help her mop the classroom floor after school. She ended up having her own class, the reception year. She's very protective of her immediate family, perhaps a little too much at times.

The area around us gradually changed for the worse. Much later, after I'd left home, my parents were out walking the dog once and they were followed by a gang of aggressive lads – high as kites – hassling them and trying to encourage a dog-fight. That was the prompt to move away.

My dad was a plumber by trade but he worked on the factory floor for British Aerospace. Cricket equipment isn't cheap, and Dad worked hard for every penny, twelve-hour shifts, days, nights. But we never went without, me and my brother.

Dad is a gentle giant. There's an edge to him, but you very rarely see it. He's got big working hands with marks all over them. When he came back from work, his hands would be a mess. He'd have a gaping wound and just stick a little plaster on it and shrug it off. At home, if he cut himself or hit his thumb with a hammer, you'd never hear a word. When he hurt his back once he was in traction for six weeks. We'd visit him in hospital in Preston and he'd be the same, making light of it. He just got on with it. That rubbed off on me. And he sticks to his principles, Dad. I looked up to him massively.

My brother was always very bright. I've got nine GCSEs. For much of my schooling I was an 'A' student. But Chris was a different level altogether academically. He was also a very talented cricketer, seriously good. That is always useful for a younger brother. You have to learn quickly to keep up. But we were different. He shied away from competition. I don't know if it was fear of failure or disliking competitiveness. I had my own issues with competitiveness – needed it, hated it.

We played cricket on the local path, even though my mum didn't like it. We'd slick up the path with a hosepipe to make the pitch play faster. We'd play over about fifteen yards, so it was pretty lively.

I broke my brother's nose once. Chris had got me out, bowled me. I threw the bat. I didn't mean to throw it *at* him, but he turned round and it hit him flush on the nose. My mum and dad were out, so we went round my mate's house, Chris's nose gushing blood. He needed an operation. I was definitely in the bad books at home that time. Chris still reminds me about it to this day.

\* \* \*

Word got around that I was a talented cricketer and I was offered sports scholarships at some of the best private schools in England. Mum would go and have a look on my behalf. I just said straight no – no chance. My school started at twenty to nine and I could be back home watching *Dallas* on UK Gold at 3 p.m. It was perfect.

Anyway, I enjoyed beating those schools too much when I played for Lancashire Schools or the North of England representative sides. The private-school lads would have brilliant, expensive kit, whereas I'd have a pair of fifteen-quid pads that my aunty got in a sale at Hamley's.

It's not a criticism of my family at all, but it still isn't obvious to me where my ambition came from. With a lot of working-class northern families, I think it comes down to 'This is what I do, this is my life,' and they're happy with it. They're not always searching for the next job or promotion. They can appreciate what they have. I respect that. But I am wired a bit differently. Only now am I starting to enjoy the important things.

Someone asked me a good but difficult question the other day. If a professional gambler had been told to bet on whether Andrew Flintoff would make it as an international cricketer – with a view just to making money, totally cold, no emotional connection at all – how would he have placed his bet?

The answer? It depends when he'd looked at me.

At eleven, put your house on it.

At thirteen, don't even waste a penny.

At fifteen, again, it's looking a good bet.

At seventeen, it's fifty–fifty.

At twenty, oh no. That's a bad bet.

At twenty-one, all bets are off. The bookies are paying out to people who had gambled on 'No, Flintoff ain't making it.'

I was like a kid in a candy store at that point. Couldn't resist the goodies. I'd celebrate anything. And I'd celebrate it with anyone. I look back at myself then and think, 'What a dick.' But at the time, I was having the time of my life, a fat lad having a laugh.

One thing that did annoy me during that period was the freeloaders who hung around but never chipped in with the bill. So many times, people would rock up after a game and enjoy the night out. But it was often me who stood the bill. I'm not talking about my mates in Preston. They always stood their round, even though they didn't have much money. It was the people who could actually afford it who milked it for all it was worth.

Looking back at those early days when I started earning a bit of cash, there's something I feel really bad about.

My dad worked so hard for every penny he earned, yet there I was just chucking it away, playing Jack the Lad, paying God knows what for a bottle of vodka or a crappy car. He must have thought, 'What on earth are you doing?'

# 3

# BLUE CAP, RED ROSE

I F someone doesn't know me – if I'm in a taxi, say – chances are that within thirty seconds they'll bring up the open-top bus ride after the Ashes or the 'Fredalo'. That's all they want to talk about. Two escapades, both fuelled by drink, one in celebration, the other a form of escape from bad times.

But there's another post-match story, away from public view, that would actually tell them a lot more about me. Picture five lads sitting in a groundsman's hut at midnight, everyone still in working clothes – I'm in whites and cricket boots – drinking beer and talking about the old days. It was at Old Trafford after the great Test match in 2005. For me, that was far better than any open-top bus trip. Everyone in that hut had known me since the beginning; they'd seen me all the way through. No acting, no persona, no showing off, no revelations.

I've played for five professional cricket teams, all told:

Lancashire, England, the ICC World XI, Chennai Super Kings and Brisbane Heat. I played at my best for only two of them, the first two. There is a reason for that. I couldn't just turn it on at will. There had to be a personal connection, a sense of meaning.

In my early teens, I went to Old Trafford to see a Rest of the World match. The ground looked so big. When someone hit a six, it was like, 'Wow, he's cleared the ropes at Old Trafford.' Then, aged fifteen, I went to one day of a Test match. We watched Pakistan play England. Wasim Akram, who was also Lancashire's overseas pro, was leading the attack for Pakistan. I never imagined that in a year's time I'd be in the same side as the man I was watching from my position of total anonymity in the stands. I was closer than I thought.

Lancashire cricket had got into my blood when I was nine. My dad was captain of the Second XI at the local club. He looked after the ground, painted the sightscreens, did everything, along with Uncle Ted and my grandpa. When I was eight or nine, a Lancashire coach came to the club and told my dad to put me in for a Lancashire trial. I was on the road.

So we went to a trial match just outside Liverpool, at

a primary school. I can't really remember how it went, but I had a phone call asking me to go to another one. After that second trial, the team's two managers got all the kids who'd played to sit on the grass. If your name was called out, you were discarded, you had to walk off.

Not great child psychology.

It was like being evicted from a reality TV show, only you were a little kid. I remember thinking, 'I'd love to get picked, but it's not happening.' When they had read the last name out and I was still sat there, it sank in. I'd been picked to represent Lancashire. I was given my first jumper and shirt, and I played for three years in the Under-11s.

The Under-11s played in the ESCA festival at Dartford in Kent. Again, I didn't expect to make the squad. At the end of the season, there was a presentation at Lancashire and Ronnie Irani, who was a young pro then, handed out special caps to all those who'd been picked, including me. It was the first time I'd had a real county cap, a Lancashire cap. It's sky blue, not navy like the full Lancashire XI cap. But it's got the same red rose.

I didn't take it off my head for weeks. I wore it in the house, wore it everywhere. I think it was then that I realised how much I had craved a Lancashire cap. There's not much cricket memorabilia in my house these days. But I can always put my hand on that cap in seconds.

It's funny, how I feel about my caps. I don't get a buzz out of just looking at them now. But when I put one on my head something inside me kicks in. A signal, a wake-up to the cricketer. When I walked out to play cricket wearing a cap – either the Lancashire rose or the three England lions – I became somebody else. It's like Clark Kent. He takes off his glasses in a phone box and comes out in his cape and underpants. That's what the caps and jumpers did for me. On England duty, I liked to wear the navy cloth cap, the real thing, during team warm-ups, just running and stretching on the outfield. That sent Duncan Fletcher mad, because we were supposed to wear the sponsor's baseball cap.

Even now, I'll take any excuse to wear the England jumper with the three lions, the proper old-school knitted one. Two years ago, long after I'd finished with England, I wore it when my brother organised a game for the people who used to play at my first club. Some might say it's embarrassing, really, to wear your England jumper to a get-together for old friends. The kind of thing you'd tease other people for doing. But I just love wearing it. I think the modern England jumpers are disgraceful, terrible things – they look like they're made of polyester. I wouldn't fancy a career in one of those. We all have moments when we imagine being in charge of English cricket. My first decision: bring back proper jumpers.

I played for Lancashire juniors all the way through. I wasn't the best player. Phil Neville was. He was an all-rounder and a year older than me. Phil used to open the batting and then open the bowling, and he was so good that often I'd resign myself to the fact that I'd probably only field that game.

Phil got offered a £2,500-a-year contract with Lancashire. Or £5,000 a week to play football for Manchester United. He took his money at United and I took his £2,500 contract at Lancashire. I sometimes wonder if the Lancashire chief executive just tippexed out 'Neville' and wrote 'Flintoff' in biro at the top of the contract. So I was pleased Phil went to play football!

It was David Lloyd, or 'Bumble', who came round to my house to sign me. We sat in the front room. There's my mum and dad, there's me on a chair and David on the sofa with the Lancashire cricket chairman, Geoff Ogden. My mum brought out all the best teacups and the special teapot and handed round the custard creams.

David told my mum and dad about Lancashire's wage structure: 'Ian Austin, he's got a second-team cap, so he gets £16,500 a year.' And you could see my mum and dad's faces: '£16,500 – amazing!' They had no idea you could get that much playing cricket.

David went on: 'Michael Atherton, he gets £28,000 a year.' And everyone was thinking, £28,000? How good is this!'

Then he said, 'And we're going to start Andrew on £2,500 a year.'

£2,500? Yes! I'd be getting paid!

David carried on with this big speech about Lancashire and its traditions and its history. I was going to be part of all that, he explained, this greater family.

I'd done my GCSEs by then, though I was still waiting on my results. My mum wanted me to go to college, but I didn't want to go. So I said, 'Look, it's a three-year contract. I'll be nineteen at the end. If this cricket thing falls apart, I'll go back to school.'

The next day I saw Bumble again. 'You've decided, haven't you?' he said. I said I had. 'One last thing,' David added in his mischievous way. 'All that stuff I told your mum and dad yesterday. Absolute rubbish. The truth? It's hard here. And it's going to be hard for you.'

\* \* \*

Bumble was all over me from the beginning. But in a good way. I didn't want to do anything to upset him. It was almost like having a second dad. I didn't drink, I didn't go out with the lads, I didn't do much at all – because I didn't want to let Bumble down.

I made my First XI debut at Portsmouth when I was sixteen. It was an embarrassing start. Bumble told the captain that I had to field in the slips: 'He catches everything, he's brilliant, he catches pigeons.' Of course, the slips were usually for the old pros, not some sixteen-year-old upstart. Neil Fairbrother was moved out to third slip so I could slot in at second. First over from Wasim Akram, I dropped one. No, I didn't even drop it. I didn't get my hands to it. Hit me in the chest, it was going so fast. Then I dropped two more. Wasim was going crazy. He eventually boomed, 'Get that boy out of the slips. Or I'll throw him a ------- pigeon.'

Early in my career I didn't always control my temper. After getting out once, I punched the wall and broke my hand. It had to be pinned. By then, Bumble had moved on to be the England coach. But he soon found out and told me straight off that I had to tell the new Lancashire coach, Dav Whatmore. When I told Dav, he wasn't that bothered. In fact, I think he was pleased I was out of the side.

When I next saw Bumble he said, 'That wasn't very clever, was it, punching a wall?' He just looked at me. He didn't have to say anything else. My heart sank, telling him I'd done something wrong. That summed up our relationship. He was an amazing supporter and influence. I hated letting him down.

When I walked into the Lancashire dressing room as a sixteen-year-old, I was really quiet. I didn't say anything. I spoke when I was spoken to. A few players seemed to be suspicious of any promising young player, always thinking about their own jobs. But lads like Fairbrother, Mike Watkinson and Wasim, they backed me, they wanted me to do well. And I sensed that. Although I didn't feel like one of them for a long time, it wasn't because of their behaviour or any coolness. It was just that I looked up to them and thought they were so much better than me. The sense of distance came from that alone. I aspired to be one of them.

In my early days at Lancashire, it was actually the Second XI where you didn't get treated so well. The atmosphere at that time was an absolute disgrace. For some reason, my closest friend Paddy McKeown and I had played against Lancashire Second XI when we were fifteen. They just abused us in that match. It was awful. And then all of a sudden I went to play for them and they thought everything would be just fine. It doesn't work like that. I played well in one game and I remember one of the old hands reassuring me that I was OK now: I'd been 'accepted' by him. I felt like saying, 'Mate, you're a thirty-year-old man. You still play in the second team. And you're asking me to seek your "acceptance"?'

One thing that deepened my relationship with Lancashire was working in the club offices in the winter. Aged sixteen I had a back problem. The only way I could have earned a living in the winter was doing manual labour or playing cricket in Australia or South Africa. Understandably, Lancashire didn't want me to do either in case my back got worse. So they gave me a job working on accounts. That didn't last long. If you did a careers profile for my character, I don't think 'accountant' would come very high up the list. I was moved down to the ticket office. It was brilliant. There was a lady called Connie, and she was like gold.

Peter Marron, the head groundsman, was asked if he would put up this sixteen-year-old lad who couldn't drive.

Pete's house was on the ground. Pete just said, 'You'll be good?' I said, 'Yes.' And he nodded.

To start with, I was a bit scared of Pete. And I wasn't sure if he really wanted me in his house, so I didn't feel comfortable sitting downstairs or watching the telly. But one Sunday, he said, 'Right, we're going to the pub. Get your coat.'

It was a pretty rough pub. When he asked me what I was going to drink, I said I'd just have a Coke. Pete shook his head at that idea. 'It's bitter or lager. You can't have Coke.' So he got me a lager. I didn't like it and I nursed it as long as possible.

The social world in the pub was so removed from what I'd experienced. One fella had been beaten up by a rival gang. Then there was some kind of love triangle going on between the barmaid, her lesbian lover and the lad who owned the pub. To me, a sixteen-year-old, it was all totally bizarre.

The following Sunday, Pete wasn't at home, so I assumed he was round the pub and I went to find him. But Pete wasn't there and I ended up sitting in the bar for about two and a half hours. I had five or six pints before Pete found out where I was. After that we got on really well, he looked after me. I think the fact his mates at the pub reckoned I was all right made all the difference.

In the office, Connie and Val and Kath, they'd mother me, make me food every evening. But then I managed to get sacked from the ticket office and they packed me off to the club shop. I loved that job. Nobody ever came in. We'd just chat all day.

Working at the club in the winter gave me a different view of what really matters. A club isn't just the players. It's not the team, or the coaches or the committee. It's everyone. You could see what Lancashire meant to the people I was working with, how they'd look forward to the season, plan the coach trips to away games. They'd talk about Lancashire all the time. What I learnt was that it is much more than just a job. You're affecting people's lives; the supporters are in it just as much as the players. It's bigger than the game on the pitch. It's a way of life, a community. And I got that.

I really enjoyed that time, working at the club shop, living with Pete. I got a girlfriend who lived in Chorlton. I'd have to creep up the stairs at Pete's house when I got back late after seeing her. I knew there was one creaky stair, but at half four in the morning I could never remember which one. Years later, Pete told me I woke him every time.

* * *

I still get a thrill, driving into Old Trafford, even today, and I always will. In 2014 I played a couple of Lancashire Second XI games when I was making my comeback. Even at thirty-seven, if I said something wrong in front of John Stanworth, who had been my first senior coach, I would feel like I was fifteen again. Not just because he'd still jump on me, but because I respect him so much.

One thing that upsets me is how impersonal Old Trafford has become. You used to go in and say hello to the man on the gate, have a quick chat, then you'd go through reception and chat to someone else there. And that wasn't just me – that was how it was for fans too. But Lancashire, like a lot of counties, seem to be losing all that, replacing it with a series of electronic barriers and car-parking systems. They are in danger of losing that human touch. Because that's what cricket is all about, when you strip things right back: people finding meaning in something.

Lancashire have sacked some of the people who've been there for ever, the soul of the club. They got rid of a fella called Ken Grime, someone I worked with in the offices. He was operation manager on match days, been there thirty-five years. He could tell you every Lancashire game that's happened in the past fifty years. I understand that cricket clubs have to move with the times and I know that it's business. But these people are the foundations and the fabric of the club, what it's all about. Get rid of the chairmen, the chief exec and the players – get rid of anyone before sacking these people. I've said my piece on all this to the club, and even though I'm never going to fall out with them, I do worry they risk losing some of the things about cricket that make it different and special.

I only fully appreciated how much Lancashire mattered to my cricket – at the sharp end – much later. When I played in the Indian Premier League, when I played that stupid Stanford game, I realised something central about my relationship with cricket, about getting the best out of myself.

I don't play for money. I'm not sure I even *can* play just for money. Money is great, I can't lie about that. But when I played for Chennai, I couldn't name everyone in my own team and coaching staff, to be honest. I only played three games. I remember standing in the middle of the field, in a yellow kit, and my body was sore and hurting, as usual, but I just couldn't put everything on the line for Chennai. It's not a reflection on them. It's not their fault. It's simply that the team didn't mean so much to me. To that extent, I'm not really a professional, in the narrow sense of the term. I can't perform to order. Some people can and that's fine. But there needs to be a reason for me.

I needed a red rose on my head or three lions. Partly it was because I was so proud to play for Lancashire and England. That goes deep. But it was also bound up with friendship, being out there with my mates, people like Neil Fairbrother, Glen Chapple, Steve Harmison and Rob Key. I was playing for everyone who'd put faith in me, so it was about loyalty to them as well as playing for myself.

The IPL? Nah. I'd always reckoned I could turn on adrenaline. But I can see now that I couldn't. There had to be an emotional attachment to what I was doing. And it had to matter. Even for England, if I went in to bat against Zimbabwe with 400 already on the board, I'd be telling myself, 'Come on, get up for it.' But something deeper would say, 'No, this is pointless.' Same thing with being a mercenary. I just couldn't get into it.

Throughout my career, the one constant has been Lancashire. But sometimes when I played for them between England games, the strength of feeling for the club could backfire. I almost felt that I should be winning every game I played and put myself under too much pressure because it meant that much. But whether I was getting a kicking in the press or playing badly, I knew I could come back to Lancashire and be surrounded by people who had always supported me. Whatever trouble I was in, playing for Lancashire gave me a way out and a way forward. Sometimes when you're struggling, it isn't advice or a strategy that you really need. It's being accepted, being with people who understand you. With that, you can turn the corner without even realising how you did it or how it happened.

When I retired from cricket, one thing that hurt was that my body hadn't allowed me to play out the end of my career with a few full seasons at Lancashire. That would have given my career the proper shape. It would have felt right, like I'd come home.

Ambition is a funny thing. In cricket, as in many professions, it tends to take you on a journey away from where you started. That's fine, maybe inevitable. But no one ever tells you that the biggest days aren't always the best days. And the richest prizes aren't always the ones you remember.

I won some winners' medals with Lancashire – a NatWest trophy and a couple of Sunday Leagues. But I desperately wanted to win the County Championship and also to win at Lord's with them one more time. Because those were the best days. And I could never have had too many with Lancashire. That's not nostalgia, just the truth.

# 4

# OLD ENGLAND,
# NEW ENGLAND

As a kid I remember my dad being on strike at work. He stuck it out all the way through, maybe for eight or nine months. There was no money coming in, we had absolutely nothing. My dad sticks to his principles. I think I inherited that trait. If I don't agree with something I'll say so, even if it's against my own interests.

I made plenty of mistakes in my early career with England. But some of the friction came from me sticking up for what I believed in. It was a strange, insecure dressing room in those days. At times, I would deliberately place myself at odds with people who seemed to be playing the system for their own benefit.

For my first England Test match at Trent Bridge in 1998 I got changed with the dressing-room attendant, in a separate little room with a washing machine in it. Making young players feel at home wasn't a top priority for the England team back then.

At Lancashire, having the support of the senior core of the team – Neil Fairbrother, Wasim Akram, Mike Watkinson – had made a massive difference to my confidence. With England in 1998, it was nothing like that. Some of the players made little attempt to hide their coldness and self-absorption. They were resentful of other players' success. I never really got a sense that we were all in it together and that we were all trying to win. The conversations were always 'He's got this sponsorship deal . . . he's got that deal . . . I want to be man of the match . . . I want this, I want that.' It wasn't a team in the proper sense of the word.

It was a big disappointment. After all those years of watching your heroes on TV, and this is how they behave? People say Kevin Pietersen is self-absorbed. He's nothing like as bad as some England players from that era.

Everything was an internal competition, with everyone trying to outdo each other. Darren Gough was the natural leader and it was as if the others were trying to catch up with him. But Goughy did it all with an innocence and a sense of humour. There was an infectious natural-ness about him that was great to be around. Goughy was brilliant with me. I am convinced there was never a moment in his career when Goughy wanted a team-mate not to do well. Gus Fraser was the same. (At the risk of starting an old argument, quick bowlers are usually less precious.) Sadly, I can't say the same thing about everyone I played with. A lot of them were fearful and guarded. I found it really weird.

Initially, my relationship with the captain, Alec Stewart, wasn't that strong, though it did improve. I still tell him today – and he still denies it! – but I wasn't sure he wanted me in the team. He wanted Ben Hollioake instead and it was a choice between the two of us. As two Surrey men, Stewey naturally had a really close relationship with Ben.

I always got on with Ben. He had made an amazing debut in the ODIs against Australia the previous year, when he'd still been in the Under-19s. Even though we did the same job, there was nothing negative about the competitiveness between me and Ben. We were always happy for each other to do well. It is often the way. If you like someone enough and support each other, the so-called 'rivalry' need not be difficult or tense. It can be fun.

I still find it hard to believe that Ben isn't with us any more. He died in a car accident in 2002, cut off as he was entering his prime. He and his brother Adam were leaving the same family gathering. Ben drove one way, Adam the other. Ben crashed and died. At twenty-four, his life was shorter than that of any other England cricketer. It's especially hard to think about Ben, because our careers had seemed intertwined from the beginning. I've remained close to Adam – a man I respect hugely – even though we have both moved on from cricket.

There was one upside to that strange England environment. I struggled with self-confidence, and at the time I was just a kid, but even then I thought to myself, 'You know what, I'm probably a bit more together than a lot of these guys.'

Later in my career, when I was more established as a player, I did my best to stop some of the dressing-room negativity I'd experienced as a newcomer. For my part, I was actually thankful when younger lads started coming into the side. I always enjoyed that freshness and having new personalities around the place.

In my early days, I was lucky to have one or two really good mates in the team. When I'd been captain of England Under-19s, I'd struck up a friendship with Steve Harmison. We'd scarcely met when he knocked on my door one night in Pakistan at 3 a.m., asking, 'You all right to have a chat?' I said, 'Yeah, come in, mate.'

He sat in my room for an hour or so, pouring his heart out about how he needed to go home, how he didn't like being on tour. And I said, 'Just give it another day.' For a week he came to my room every night with the newspaper his mum had sent him from home.

Eventually I went to see tour manager John Abrahams, the former Lancashire player, and said, 'Look, Harmy has got to go home. This lad, he can't do it.' And he did go home. But from those moments we became such good mates. Perhaps it was because we gained each other's trust. The trust was still there when we graduated into the full England side.

The following year Rob Key came into the Under-19 side. Keysey is quick-witted, always in the thick of the mickey-taking, and never short of a one-liner. He could really play, too, especially when he was into a battle. Even at the beginning of the 2015 season – aged thirty-six, and after lots of injuries – he stood up to Mitchell Johnson while making a good 87 for Kent against the Aussies.

The three of us became thick as thieves. But I'm not sure we helped each other's careers, to be honest. We were so keen to have a laugh that while we entertained some of the lads, we probably hacked off just as many. Looking back, I can see it didn't always go down too well with those in charge. (Mates over politics: I'd take that deal every time.)

When we played in the full England team, it became obvious to me that Duncan Fletcher in particular didn't want the three of us. Not together. I came to realise that I had to play out of my skin every time otherwise I'd be dropped. I saw what happened to Keysey. He got 200 against West Indies, a 90 not out, then a couple of bad games and he was gone, out for good. Duncan never needed a second opportunity to put a line through someone he felt wasn't part of his inner circle.

So I feel a little guilty about that. My friendship with Rob probably didn't help his international prospects. But we did have some fun. And I was glad that when he had his benefit year for Kent, I could do him the odd favour.

At times the England management tried to involve me a bit more. It didn't always work out. In Australia in 2002, I was put on the management committee. In one of the meetings, Fletcher was disappointed with me for not having any input at all when we were talking about Adam Gilchrist. He was a player I'd scarcely seen and had never played against. What did he want me to say? Make it up? After that, I got the feeling that Fletcher wanted to send me home.

By then I'd also seen through the rationale for those committees. In theory, the idea was for the captain and coach to appoint a group of players – not just senior players, but drawn from across the squad – to act as a kind of think tank. In reality, it was mainly a way of telling tales on other people.

One day we were talking about Vikram Solanki, who'd had a couple of failures. Out of the blue, some of the players on the committee started writing off his mental state, saying he was shot. 'Hang on a minute. When did you do your psychology degree?' I said. 'What do you know about Vikram's head? I can't be a part of this. This is nonsense.' So I was bumped off the committee there and then.

I'd always stand up for people if I felt they were being stitched up. That's got me into so much trouble over the years. No doubt it always will. Most of the time I'm pretty relaxed and chilled out, but if I see something I don't agree with, I won't back down. That bothered some of the older players and it definitely bothered Duncan. I didn't run my opinions past him to get them rubber-stamped. I didn't play ball.

\* \* \*

37

On the field, it definitely took me a while to find my feet. I pretty much had to learn how to bowl properly while playing international cricket. For years I just hadn't been able to bowl that much because of recurrent injuries. Even before my Test debut, against South Africa in July 1998, I'd scarcely bowled in the three weeks running up to the game. I was essentially learning on the job.

My role in the team was often unclear. In my early years, I was employed in many different roles as a bowler. One day I'd be the stock bowler getting through lots of donkey work. Then they'd want me to bowl quick, in short spells. The theory was that I'd bowl about fifteen overs a day. It rarely worked out that way. It was always more.

That caused problems, too. During the home series versus India in 2002, I bowled through a double hernia for three months. I missed the last Test to have an operation with a view to being fit for the Ashes trip that winter. When I got to Perth at the start of the tour I literally could not run. This had been discussed in detail with the relevant medical staff before the tour, but at the first practice I was still pulled over to the side as I walked around the outfield.

'What's up? Why aren't you running?'

I replied, 'You know I can't run. I'm recovering from my operation.'

'What do you mean you can't run?'

'Well, the definition is when you are moving quickly enough that both feet are off the ground . . .'

'But when the medical staff told me you can't run, I didn't realise they meant you can't run.'

'So,' I said, 'what did it mean to you, then, that phrase "can't run"?'

Despite all that, I was selected for a tour game a few weeks later in Tasmania. I couldn't move afterwards. I was sent to hospital for an exploratory injection. I've suffered quite a few unpleasant medical chapters in my life, but this one was right up there.

The injection was into my pubic symphysis, a bit of cartilage between your two pubic bones – a gap above your knob, basically, where they can ram a needle in. I was lying stark naked on the hospital bed, watching in terror as a tiny Chinese doctor walked towards me with the biggest needle I've ever seen. There was a nurse either side of me. One was looking at me especially sympathetically. I did say, 'To be honest, love, it's usually a bit bigger. I'm just really nervous.'

It was the worst pain I've ever had. Didn't work, either. Before I knew it, I was back home, tour over.

\* \* \*

What about my weight? Was that part of the problem? I struggled to maintain a steady weight throughout my early career. Aged twenty, I was living on my own in Manchester and I had the pizza man on speed dial. On the field I was getting loads of abuse from the crowd about being fat. Then I'd go into the supermarket thinking everyone was watching me. I had all the usual excuses, of course. Big-boned? Think about it. Have you ever seen a fat skeleton?

My methods for losing weight were as dangerous as carrying it. I made myself sick. If I ate something that I thought I shouldn't have, I would make myself throw up. Then it began creeping in more and more. Only much later did I tell my wife, Rachael, and just the act of telling someone made it so much better.

Meanwhile, I learnt the hard way that from a purely cricketing perspective I could be too thin as well as too fat. After one bout of ankle problems, I got down to 98 kg, just to see if it helped with the ankle. Even though I was conditioned, I found I lacked strength as a bowler. I was OK for one and a half spells at decent pace. For the third and fourth spells, I had nothing.

My batting was up and down for different reasons – mental rather than physical. Confidence is the key for most batsmen, for me even more so. When I was playing well, I'd think, 'I'll hit him back over his head in a minute. Then I'll whack him over there.' If I was playing badly, I'd look around the field and just see big people in whites wanting to catch me out.

For all the bravado of striding out to bat without my helmet on, head up, big persona, maybe only twice was I really thinking, 'I'll be totally in charge out here.' Every other time, I was thinking, 'I'm not sure I can do this.' It often came down to whether I could start my innings well. Just one good shot might be enough to make me click into gear.

What could I have done to get into that mindset more often? I always had a love–hate relationship with sports psychology. Looking back, I probably should have tried more of it. After all, you spend all that time working on your body in the gym and practising in the nets. And yet the most important thing is your mind; that's the first domino.

But back then I didn't know myself in the same way. And I was easily annoyed by nonsense. I remember I saw a sports psychologist who was one of the 'positive' people. His mantra was 'Every day above ground is a good day.' No it's not. There are bad days above ground too. And when I'd played awfully in the middle he'd say, 'What about that four? That must have felt great.' Nope. I was out for seven.

I went to see another sports psychologist called Steve Peters. I thought, 'He's only down the road, works for British cycling. They're doing well. He must be good.' So I went to his house in Disley. He opened the door and sat me down in one of those Chesterfield couches in his study.

He was sitting next to a flip chart, which is never a good sign. Me and flip charts don't go well together. So we exchanged pleasantries and then he says, 'Let me tell you a bit about myself.' And off he went: 'I've won X number of gold medals. I've won this, I won that . . .'

'Hang on a second,' I said. 'Gold medals? Wow. Can I see one? Never seen a gold medal.'

'No, no, *I* haven't got any gold medals. No, no, I worked with the athletes – Chris Hoy, Victoria Pendleton and so on – and *talked* them into their gold medals . . .'

So what we're talking about is gold medals for talking? Oh great.

Then he turns to his flip chart and draws a head on it. 'Do you know what that is?'

'It's a head,' I said.

'You've got a chimp in there. You've got a chimp in your head.'

'I don't think I have,' I said. 'I think I'd know about it if I did.'

'No, you have got a chimp in your head,' he said. 'What I mean by that is that the back of your head is eight times stronger than the front bit, so the back bit takes over. But your rational thoughts and so on are at the front. So what you've got to do is take over from the chimp at the back.'

'How long is this going to go on for?' I thought. 'I want to go home.'

I did the hour with him and then I left. Perhaps Steve didn't catch me on a good day – and he is highly rated in his field – but it didn't click for me.

Everyone was asking how it went. 'Brilliant. I've got a chimp in my head.' When I played next, I got out to a horrendous shot. 'It's not my fault. It's this chimp in my head.'

The official England sports psychologist was Steve Bull, a lovely man, always got on well with him. I had many debates with him about it all. He's always open to both sides of the argument. Early on, when I was trying to lose weight, Steve said, 'What do you like eating?'

I said, 'I like chocolate. I like Mars bars.'

'Right. Well, get a carrot and visualise it's a Mars bar.'

'I can't do that, Steve,' I said. 'It's a carrot. It's orange. I put it in my mouth, I bite it – it's a carrot. All the visualising techniques in the world, they are not going to tell me that's a Mars bar. That is a carrot.'

So I was put off sports psychology at a young age. I toyed with it more later in my career and sometimes it's been helpful. On reflection, though, I don't think sports psychology is always the right term. Knowing yourself, being self-aware, that's the most important thing. You only get that through life experience, which is the hard bit. There aren't any short cuts. You have to work it out for yourself.

Collective meetings, about the 'mind' of the whole team, were even more of a waste of time. Cricket isn't like a business. It doesn't require 'a strategy'. The strategy is always the same. To win. Meeting over. Five seconds. Anyone for a spot of lunch?

In my early England days, there was a bit of tension with Nasser Hussain. On one occasion, I definitely pushed my luck.

I was great mates with Muttiah Muralitharan, dating

back to his days at Lancashire. In an England v Sri Lanka series, it panned out that I wasn't bowling too much short stuff at him and he wasn't bowling too many doosras at me. Which was a bit naughty, I can see that.

I'd had dinner with him the night before one match. Murali said, 'Fred, I haven't got any bats left. Can I borrow one of yours?' We used the same bat sponsor at the time. It was a bit tricky because Nasser had put a ban on us even talking to Murali. We were supposed to be freezing him out.

Murali tried again on the morning of the match, asking for a word. Nasser was glaring at me from a distance, clearly very unhappy. So I said to Murali as quickly as possible, 'When we go out to field, go into the England dressing rooms. Just nip in the back door and take one of my bats – but keep the whole thing under your hat.'

Once the match was under way and we took a few Sri Lankan wickets, Nasser brought me on to bowl out the tail, as was the plan in those days. Out strides Murali, carrying my bat. Nasser, meanwhile, talks me through the plan.

'I want you to go at him. Short stuff.'

Hmm. Tricky one this, on lots of levels, especially given the status of bouncers and doosras for me and Murali.

'Nasser, I think I can get a yorker through him, nice and full will do the job here.'

'No, I just told you,' he said. 'I want you to go at him.'

'No, I'm going to try and bowl him. Hit the stumps. Job done.'

So I ran in, trying to bowl a yorker, directly against instructions. Didn't get through. In fact, it found the middle of the bat, my bat – good middle it had, too.

Nasser threw all his toys out of the pram. I was taken off. Then Murali started charging the other bowlers, smashing them.

After one huge six, Murali walks between me and Nasser at the change of ends. I can see Nasser has clocked my initials on the bat. He's ready to explode.

Murali has a huge grin on his face: '------- good bat, Freddie!'

For all the comedy value, I let Nasser down that day, I can see that.

I respected Nasser's captaincy. I'm never going to be mates with him. But he was certainly totally committed to improving the England team. And it wasn't an easy time to captain England. Among that generation of England cricketers, there was almost a jealousy towards anybody who was good, especially the Australians. It was all about how the Aussies were this and that, what dicks they were. Actually, they weren't. I reckon if some of England's top players had concentrated on themselves a bit more, they might have done all right. We built up Australia too much.

Nasser was known as a tough captain. And he was. But while Steve Waugh was a tough captain because he was tough on the opposition, a lot of Nasser's toughness could be directed towards his own players. Set against that, you never doubted his passion or commitment.

His self-absorption could occasionally affect things on the pitch. In a 2002 ODI at Lord's – when India chased down 326 to win, which wasn't such a routine event back then – I batted with Nasser when we were trying to push on and raise the scoring rate. He seemed preoccupied with his hundred as well as the match situation. He did get his hundred, prompting his famous gesturing to his shirt number, the number three on his back, but we lost the match because we were 15 short.

There was something in Nasser's DNA that was grudging. That was his great strength but occasionally his weakness. It also set things up nicely for Michael Vaughan when he became captain in 2003. Nasser had gone, the shackles were off. But, along the way, Nasser had made his contribution.

Michael was a breath of fresh air. His foundation as a captain was getting to know people. With me, for example, he always gave me enough rope to hang myself. If I was pushing it, he'd let me know. He'd treat me differently to Ashley Giles, and he'd treat Gilo differently to Marcus Trescothick.

Over the course of 2003, Vaughany's influence gradually rippled through the side. Confidence grew. There was a feeling that it was becoming *our* side now. An example of that was Graham Thorpe's return to the team at The Oval for the last Test against South Africa in 2003. He was an old head, the second most experienced player in the team. But rather than us fitting in around him, he had to adapt to the way we were playing, the culture of the new side. The vibe towards him was 'We're a set of young lads and we're just having a crack at it. You've got to enjoy it, too.'

We also supported each other. Whether it was me, or Harmy, or Ashley Giles or, later, Simon Jones and Hoggy – we'd all be pleased for the guy who got the wickets. We didn't look at our figures at the end of the day and see 20 overs, no wickets for 40 as a failure. We'd take heart at how we had helped one of the other lads get his wickets. That was part of the job, part of what we enjoyed.

Gilo was among the best at that. He got a kicking from the press all the way through, partly because it is perceived to be a boring tactic for a left-armer to bowl over the wicket at right-handers. First, bowling over the wicket helped him to bowl a more dangerous line. Secondly, from the team perspective, him going for one and a half an over enabled us fast bowlers to do our jobs, to have more time to recover. He was an unsung hero.

In terms of personal form, that 2003 series against South Africa cemented a new confidence and freedom in me. My first Test hundred at home – at Lord's – was a turning point. It was a bizarre innings, which I'll come to later.

Increasingly, I wasn't thinking I was bowling as a third or fourth seamer, or that I was bowling in my capacity as an all-rounder. I was bowling as a bowler, full stop. I bowled with aggression, with conviction. There was a bit of aggro flying around as well. In that series I ended up walking out to bat shouting at Graeme Smith, before I'd even faced the ball.

The classic match at The Oval, which we won to level the series, was another big step towards finding my voice on that stage. In their first innings, South Africa were 345–2 at one point. It looked as though they were going to close out the match and take the series 2–1. The odds on an England win after the first day's play were 40–1, apparently – almost like Headingley in 1981.

Somehow we pegged them back to 484 all out, a real team effort and very typical of that bowling unit. But we still had a difficult task ahead. At that point, in the history of Test cricket, only six times had a team scored so many runs in their first innings and lost the match.

In reply, Marcus set up our first innings with a majestic double ton. But we still had to get ahead – and quickly. So when I went out to bat, there was no time to waste – and it was all kicking off out in the middle.

Makhaya Ntini was bowling, charging in. I squeezed one ball and it got stuck in my pad flap, rattled around a bit, then dropped on the batting crease right in front of me.

As a kid, I was told you never pick up the ball when you're batting. One, it's against the laws of the game. Two, you spend enough time fielding as it is. So my thinking was always: 'I'm not picking up the ball; that's what the fielders are for.' And if the ball came to rest near me, I used to stand over the bowler as he picked it up.

That's what happened this time. I stood behind the ball

and Ntini picked it up right in front of me after he'd finished his follow-through.

Suddenly Herschelle Gibbs shouted, 'Does that feel good?'

I said, 'What are you on about?'

Gibbs came back at me: 'Having a black man at your feet?'

'You've really lost me. You what?'

'A black man picking something up at your feet,' Gibbs said.

He started having a go at me for being racist, and about four or five other South African players joined in.

I said, 'Mate, you've got this completely wrong.'

The next ball was pitched up and I hit it for six.

Then I said, 'So you can go and get that one as well.'

And then next ball he dropped short and I hit it for six, too.

'You want me to get that one? Or are you going to go, Ntini?'

It was pretty lively out there. One of my sixes ended up breaking the dressing-room window. It was a check drive, just a little chip, but it kept going and going.

I was batting with Harmy. We put on 99 together and he made six. It was so much fun. Instead of thinking, 'How is my footwork? What's the bowler thinking?' I was just hitting the ball, with a simple and uncluttered mind, with a total absence of irrelevant thought. That's why, over the long term, Twenty20 will teach batsmen some important lessons. In T20 there's no time to worry about footwork or technique; you're focused on hitting the ball. That's when you strike it best.

I was trying to hit another six when I was bowled for 95. Disappointed? Well, I don't really get this obsession with personal milestones. The tide of the Test had turned, we were dominating a game when we'd been getting smashed, the crowd were on their feet, I was loving it – and I'm supposed to worry about missing out on a ton? You must be joking.

We skittled the South Africans for 229 and won the match by nine wickets, an astonishing comeback. We had established a pattern of belief and aggression that would serve us well over the next two years.

As for me, five years after my debut Test in 1998, when I'd changed next to that washing machine at Trent Bridge, I was ready to take centre stage.

# England v South Africa (5th Test)

*Played at The Oval, London, on 4–8 September 2003*

Umpires:  SJA Taufel & S Venkataraghavan (TV: JW Lloyds)
Referee:   RS Madugalle
Toss:      South Africa

## SOUTH AFRICA

| | | | | | |
|---|---|---|---|---|---|
| GC Smith* | run out (Vaughan/Stewart) | 18 | lbw b Bicknell | | 19 |
| HH Gibbs | b Giles | 183 | c Stewart b Anderson | | 9 |
| G Kirsten | lbw b Giles | 90 | c Trescothick b Harmison | | 29 |
| JH Kallis | run out (Giles) | 66 | lbw b Harmison | | 35 |
| ND McKenzie | c Stewart b Anderson | 9 | lbw b Flintoff | | 38 |
| JA Rudolph | lbw b Bicknell | 0 | b Bicknell | | 8 |
| MV Boucher† | c Stewart b Bicknell | 8 | c Stewart b Bicknell | | 25 |
| SM Pollock | not out | 66 | c Thorpe b Harmison | | 43 |
| AJ Hall | lbw b Flintoff | 1 | c Smith b Bicknell | | 0 |
| PR Adams | run out (Butcher/Giles) | 1 | not out | | 13 |
| M Ntini | b Anderson | 11 | c Smith b Harmison | | 1 |
| Extras | (b 12, lb 10, w 4, nb 5) | 31 | (b 1, lb 7, nb 1) | | 9 |
| **Total** | (128 overs) | **484** | (69.2 overs) | | **229** |

## ENGLAND

| | | | | | |
|---|---|---|---|---|---|
| ME Trescothick | c Rudolph b Ntini | 219 | not out | | 69 |
| MP Vaughan* | c Gibbs b Pollock | 23 | c Boucher b Kallis | | 13 |
| MA Butcher | lbw b Hall | 32 | not out | | 20 |
| GP Thorpe | b Kallis | 124 | | | |
| ET Smith | lbw b Hall | 16 | | | |
| AJ Stewart† | lbw b Pollock | 38 | | | |
| A Flintoff | b Adams | 95 | | | |
| AF Giles | c Hall b Kallis | 2 | | | |
| MP Bicknell | lbw b Pollock | 0 | | | |
| SJ Harmison | not out | 6 | | | |
| JM Anderson | not out | 0 | | | |
| Extras | (b 11, lb 18, w 9, nb 11) | 49 | (lb 4, nb 4) | | 8 |
| **Total** | (for 9 wkts dec) (162 overs) | **604** | (for 1 wkt) (22.2 overs) | | **110** |

| ENGLAND | O | M | R | W | | O | M | R | W | Fall of wickets: | | | | |
|---|---|---|---|---|---|---|---|---|---|---|---|---|---|---|
| Bicknell | 20 | 3 | 71 | 2 | | 24 | 5 | 84 | 4 | | SA | Eng | SA | Eng |
| Anderson | 25 | 6 | 86 | 2 | | 10 | 1 | 55 | 1 | 1st | 63 | 28 | 24 | 47 |
| Harmison | 27 | 8 | 73 | 0 | | 19.2 | 8 | 33 | 4 | 2nd | 290 | 78 | 34 | – |
| Giles | 29 | 3 | 102 | 2 | | 10 | 2 | 36 | 0 | 3rd | 345 | 346 | 92 | – |
| Flintoff | 19 | 4 | 88 | 1 | | 6 | 2 | 13 | 1 | 4th | 362 | 379 | 93 | – |
| Vaughan | 5 | 0 | 24 | 0 | | | | | | 5th | 365 | 480 | 118 | – |
| Butcher | 3 | 0 | 18 | 0 | | | | | | 6th | 385 | 489 | 150 | – |
| | | | | | | | | | | 7th | 419 | 502 | 193 | – |
| SOUTH AFRICA | O | M | R | W | | O | M | R | W | 8th | 421 | 502 | 193 | – |
| Pollock | 39 | 10 | 111 | 3 | | 6 | 0 | 15 | 0 | 9th | 432 | 601 | 215 | – |
| Ntini | 31 | 4 | 129 | 1 | | 8 | 0 | 46 | 0 | 10th | 484 | – | 229 | – |
| Hall | 35 | 5 | 111 | 2 | | | | | | | | | | |
| Kallis | 34 | 5 | 117 | 2 | (3) | 5.2 | 0 | 25 | 1 | | | | | |
| Adams | 17 | 2 | 79 | 1 | (4) | 3 | 0 | 20 | 0 | | | | | |
| Rudolph | 6 | 1 | 28 | 0 | | | | | | | | | | |

Close of play:     Day 1: SA (1) 362–4 (Kallis 32*, 89.5 overs)
                    Day 2: Eng (1) 165–2 (Trescothick 64*, Thorpe 28*, 46 overs)
                    Day 3: Eng (1) 502–7 (Flintoff 10*, Bicknell 0*, 140 overs)
                    Day 4: SA (2) 185–6 (Boucher 22*, Pollock 19*, 57 overs)

Man of the Match: ME Trescothick
**Result:**          **England won by 9 wickets**

# 5

# INSIDE THE GREATEST SERIES

John Crawley spoke to me before the 2005 Ashes. His message was simple: 'They'll come at you hard when you bat, Fred.' I was going to get peppered with short stuff every time I walked out to bat. .

In the Twenty20 before the Test series, I was bowling when Brett Lee – the fastest bowler in their team – came out to bat. I thought, 'Sod it, I'm going to get in first here.' I just went at him. I hit him on the shoulder. Brett went off the field and missed the start of the one-day series with the injury.

But at Lord's, the first Test of the series, I bottled it. Completely bottled it.

I'd never done that before, or at least not for years. I hadn't bottled it to that extent since childhood days. Acknowledging that fact, facing up to what went wrong at Lord's, spurred me to play differently for the rest of the series. Losing the first Test like that really hit me hard. I didn't know what had happened. But it turned out that the important failure had come at the right moment in the summer. It was time for a proper rethink about myself and my game, and a pretty quick rethink at that.

Before the first Test I was playing really well and – without blowing my own trumpet – I knew I was a big player in the team. I also knew that as an England player you get judged on your performances against Australia. I'm usually good at removing outside pressures (I don't really read newspapers), but before the 2005 Ashes something got into my system. I started saying to myself, 'I've got to do this . . . I've got to do that.' That was not a voice I should ever have listened to.

We bowled first at Lord's. I was out of control. And I don't mean a lack of line-and-length control. My eyes had gone. I didn't know what I was doing out there, and I couldn't do anything about it. I got a couple of wickets but that didn't tell the real story.

Before I went in to bat, it was even worse. Usually I'm messing around a bit, disorganised, just in my underpants until I'm actually the next man in. Even then, I'll be making a brew and chatting to Harmy about some nonsense.

Not at Lord's in 2005. Well in advance, I had the lot on, even my helmet, ready to go in. People said, 'Take your helmet off!' So I did. Only to put it straight back on again. When the moment came to bat, I went out and got a duck. Yes, it was a good ball from McGrath, nipped back and hit off-stump. But the expression on my face in the photos is oddly resigned. 'Oddly resigned' is a bad expression. OK, it was a good ball. But if I'd been forward trying to hit the ball, it wouldn't have got me out.

Second innings, same story. In the field: eyes gone, dropped a catch, hands too firm. With the bat: Shane Warne caught me off one of his flippers. I went back, which is fatal. (By the way, 'mystery' has nothing to do with it. He might as well tell you he's going to bowl it. It's not a mystery. That doesn't mean you can play it, though.) When I went back and was caught behind, Ricky Ponting had a good sledge for me. I was in with Kevin, and the Aussies were on top. Kevin and I used the same bat sponsor. From right under my nose, Ponting says from silly point, 'I bet your sponsor's happy with you two -----.' Fair dos, Rick, well said.

When I was out and got back to the dressing room, I just sat there. It was almost a relief that the game was over. Not good. Not me. Or at least the wrong me.

I hadn't prepared myself for how big the Ashes was. Lord's felt like making my Test debut all over again and I am terrible at debuts – all my debuts have gone really badly. This extra debut was no exception.

One thing stayed with me from Lord's, even though I had a bad game: walking through the Long Room on the first day. I'm torn about the Long Room, to be honest. I don't want to like it. Some of the old duffers are just everything that I'd never want to be. But there's something about the place that I can't help liking, despite myself.

Walking through on that first day was crazy. You've got dozens of seventy-year-old men in ties and hats whacking on the barrier, shouting, 'RAAAAAAGH!' If you can imagine five hundred very posh, very sophisticated football hooligans, that's what they were like. And it was brilliant, like nothing I'd ever experienced before. And I thought to myself, 'Bloody hell, look at these lads here, they're up for it!'

After that first Test I had to sort out my mind. Instead of going home, me and the family went to Devon, to Bovey Castle. I didn't train at all. I didn't pick up a bat or a ball for a week. I drank cider, had some red wine, smoked a few cigars, chatted things through with the missus and some close friends. And eventually I came to the following conclusion: 'You know what, if it's going to go well, great, enjoy it. If it's going to go bad, it's going to go bad on my terms. At least I'm going to have a go, I'm going to enjoy it.'

I arranged to meet up with a different psychologist when we got home. He came round to our house and he had me doing my run-up in the garden. Rachael was looking out of the window, probably thinking, 'What's going on? Has he gone mad?'

I marked out my run-up on the lawn with Jamie walking next to me – not easy, as I had to snake the run-up around the kids' climbing frame. The exercise was about never looking down. Never look down, always look up, keep looking up. And it was about visualisation. And that was something I could understand – never looking down, never yielding an advantage, never conceding ground. Look up. Visualise you are a giant. You're in this field and you're just bigger and taller and faster and stronger than anyone else.

I never really told anyone about all that. It's certainly not the kind of subject that I rush to discuss with the lads. But after a while I started doing it and it felt comfortable.

\* \* \*

Off to Edgbaston, then, for the second Test, this time with a bit of a spring in my step. But it was Marcus Trescothick who changed the series. When we were put in to bat by Ponting, Marcus started off brilliantly, just smashing them everywhere. It might only read 90 in the scorebook but Marcus's knock was worth vastly more than many big hundreds. It announced that we had come to play.

When I came in at number six, my Test match was up and running straight away. Luck played its hand, as it so often does. I squeezed a four just over Kasprowicz's outstretched hand at mid-off. A few inches lower and he would have caught it and I would have suffered three failures out of three. It was a *Sliding Doors* moment. An innings, a match, a series, a career: so much hinges on chance. If he'd timed his jump better, it would have been a different game – maybe an entirely different series. Much as I like to think I could have put three failures behind me and that England would eventually have forced our way into the series, in truth you can never be absolutely certain.

As things turned out, I managed to clear the ropes a couple of times early on, the first one over long-on. Then I flicked one over midwicket for six, which I didn't mean to do. That was when I thought, 'I'm in here.' And things just started happening. It all came back. I was enjoying it again. I wasn't worrying about who was bowling at me. I just wanted to get on strike and bat against them. I was into the match and into the series. What I had neglected until then was that batting isn't about fretting over your footwork, it's about where you are mentally. And that refound freedom and confidence also flowed into my bowling.

After we'd won at Edgbaston, there was that photo of me consoling Brett Lee, who'd batted so bravely but ended up on the losing side. A lot was made of it. I'd just add two things. First, Harmy shook Brett's hand before I did. But nobody got that photograph, so it didn't become an iconic image. Secondly, I think sport is in a sad state of affairs when a gesture like that gets so much air time. It's just something you should really do. Has sportsman-ship reached such a low level that someone putting an arm around an opponent or shaking his hand has become national news? It was no different to what we got taught as kids at Lancashire. 'Unlucky, Brett, see you next week.' I wouldn't have said any more than that.

Other moments I remember best from 2005 are often surprisingly ordinary, as though I drank in every moment

# England v Australia (2nd Test)

*Played at Edgbaston, Birmingham, on 4–7 August 2005*

Umpires: BF Bowden & RE Koertzen (TV: JW Lloyds)
Referee: RS Madugalle
Toss: Australia

## ENGLAND

| | | | | | |
|---|---|---|---|---|---|
| ME Trescothick | c Gilchrist b Kasprowicz | 90 | | c Gilchrist b Lee | 21 |
| AJ Strauss | b Warne | 48 | | b Warne | 6 |
| MP Vaughan* | c Lee b Gillespie | 24 | (4) | b Lee | 1 |
| IR Bell | c Gilchrist b Kasprowicz | 6 | (5) | c Gilchrist b Warne | 21 |
| KP Pietersen | c Katich b Lee | 71 | (6) | c Gilchrist b Warne | 20 |
| A Flintoff | c Gilchrist b Gillespie | 68 | (7) | b Warne | 73 |
| GO Jones† | c Gilchrist b Kasprowicz | 1 | (8) | c Ponting b Lee | 9 |
| AF Giles | lbw b Warne | 23 | (9) | c Hayden b Warne | 8 |
| MJ Hoggard | lbw b Warne | 16 | (3) | c Hayden b Lee | 1 |
| SJ Harmison | b Warne | 17 | | c Ponting b Warne | 0 |
| SP Jones | not out | 19 | | not out | 12 |
| Extras | (lb 9, w 1, nb 14) | 24 | | (lb 1, nb 9) | 10 |
| **Total** | (79.2 overs) | **407** | | (52.1 overs) | **82** |

## AUSTRALIA

| | | | | | |
|---|---|---|---|---|---|
| JL Langer | lbw b SP Jones | 82 | | b Flintoff | 28 |
| ML Hayden | c Strauss b Hoggard | 0 | | c Trescothick b SP Jones | 31 |
| RT Ponting* | c Vaughan b Giles | 61 | | c GO Jones b Flintoff | 0 |
| DR Martyn | run out (Vaughan) | 20 | | c Bell b Hoggard | 28 |
| MJ Clarke | c GO Jones b Giles | 40 | | b Harmison | 30 |
| SM Katich | c GO Jones b Flintoff | 4 | | c Trescothick b Giles | 16 |
| AC Gilchrist† | not out | 49 | | c Flintoff b Giles | 1 |
| SK Warne | b Giles | 8 | (9) | hit wicket b Flintoff | 42 |
| B Lee | c Flintoff b SP Jones | 6 | (10) | not out | 43 |
| JN Gillespie | lbw b Flintoff | 7 | (8) | lbw b Flintoff | 0 |
| MS Kasprowicz | lbw b Flintoff | 0 | | c GO Jones b Harmison | 20 |
| Extras | (b 13, lb 7, w 1, nb 10) | 31 | | (b 13, lb 8, w 1, nb 18) | 40 |
| **Total** | (76 overs) | **308** | | (64.3 overs) | **279** |

| AUSTRALIA | O | M | R | W | | O | M | R | W | | Fall of wickets: | | | | |
|---|---|---|---|---|---|---|---|---|---|---|---|---|---|---|---|
| Lee | 17 | 1 | 111 | 1 | | 18 | 1 | 82 | 4 | | | Eng | Aus | Eng | Aus |
| Gillespie | 22 | 3 | 91 | 2 | | 8 | 0 | 24 | 0 | | 1st | 112 | 0 | 25 | 47 |
| Kasprowicz | 15 | 3 | 80 | 3 | | 3 | 0 | 29 | 0 | | 2nd | 164 | 88 | 27 | 48 |
| Warne | 25.2 | 4 | 116 | 4 | | 23.1 | 7 | 46 | 6 | | 3rd | 170 | 118 | 29 | 82 |
| | | | | | | | | | | | 4th | 187 | 194 | 31 | 107 |
| ENGLAND | O | M | R | W | | O | M | R | W | | 5th | 290 | 208 | 72 | 134 |
| Harmison | 11 | 1 | 48 | 0 | | 17.3 | 3 | 62 | 2 | | 6th | 293 | 262 | 75 | 136 |
| Hoggard | 8 | 0 | 41 | 1 | | 5 | 0 | 26 | 1 | | 7th | 342 | 273 | 101 | 137 |
| SP Jones | 16 | 2 | 69 | 2 | (5) | 5 | 1 | 23 | 1 | | 8th | 348 | 282 | 131 | 175 |
| Flintoff | 15 | 1 | 52 | 3 | | 22 | 3 | 79 | 4 | | 9th | 375 | 308 | 131 | 220 |
| Giles | 26 | 2 | 78 | 3 | (3) | 15 | 3 | 68 | 2 | | 10th | 407 | 308 | 182 | 279 |

Close of play:  Day 1: Eng (1) 407
Day 2: Eng (2) 25–1 (Trescothick 19*, Hoggard 0*, 7 overs)
Day 3: Aus (2) 175–8 (Warne 20*, 43.4 overs)

Man of the Match: A Flintoff
**Result:**  **England won by 2 runs**

of normal life that I could. The Edgbaston Test match finished on the Sunday morning. At 2 p.m., Glenn Chapple's daughter was having a birthday party. So I was on the clock a bit once the game had finished, thinking to myself, 'Let's get these interviews done, I've got to get to Chappy's house.'

Within two hours, I was sat with Chappy in his back garden with a can of beer, watching the kids playing. In a way, I didn't know what had happened really, the drama of that Edgbaston victory. Life just carried on. It didn't get spoken about much at Chappy's. We said, yeah, that was all right. Then it was, 'You got any chocolate fingers?' It was understated, normal, nice.

The third Test, on home turf at Old Trafford, is one of my favourite cricket matches. Seeing Lancashire's ground at its best, totally full, with all those supporters desperate to get in, my family and friends all there, as well as the people I'd worked with at the club – that all meant so much to me.

After the game, a tense draw, I didn't want to head into town with the other players. I was last out of the dressing room. That was when I made my way over to the groundsman's hut. We sat there – me, Pete Marron

# England v Australia (3rd Test)

*Played at Old Trafford, Manchester, on 11–15 August 2005*

Umpires: BF Bowden & SA Bucknor (TV: NJ Llong)
Referee: RS Madugalle
Toss: England

## ENGLAND

| | | | | | |
|---|---|---|---|---|---|
| ME Trescothick | c Gilchrist b Warne | 63 | | b McGrath | 41 |
| AJ Strauss | b Lee | 6 | | c Martyn b McGrath | 106 |
| MP Vaughan* | c McGrath b Katich | 166 | | c sub (BJ Hodge) b Lee | 14 |
| IR Bell | c Gilchrist b Lee | 59 | | c Katich b McGrath | 65 |
| KP Pietersen | c sub (BJ Hodge) b Lee | 21 | | lbw b McGrath | 0 |
| MJ Hoggard | b Lee | 4 | | | |
| A Flintoff | c Langer b Warne | 46 | (6) | b McGrath | 4 |
| GO Jones† | b Gillespie | 42 | (7) | not out | 27 |
| AF Giles | c Hayden b Warne | 0 | (8) | not out | 0 |
| SJ Harmison | not out | 10 | | | |
| SP Jones | b Warne | 0 | | | |
| Extras | (b 4, lb 5, w 3, nb 15) | 27 | | (b 5, lb 3, w 1, nb 14) | 23 |
| Total | (113.2 overs) | 444 | | (for 6 wkts dec) (61.5 overs) | 280 |

## AUSTRALIA

| | | | | | |
|---|---|---|---|---|---|
| JL Langer | c Bell b Giles | 31 | | c GO Jones b Hoggard | 14 |
| ML Hayden | lbw b Giles | 34 | | b Flintoff | 36 |
| RT Ponting* | c Bell b SP Jones | 7 | | c GO Jones b Harmison | 156 |
| DR Martyn | b Giles | 20 | | lbw b Harmison | 19 |
| SM Katich | b Flintoff | 17 | | c Giles b Flintoff | 12 |
| AC Gilchrist† | c GO Jones b SP Jones | 30 | | c Bell b Flintoff | 4 |
| SK Warne | c Giles b SP Jones | 90 | (9) | c GO Jones b Flintoff | 34 |
| MJ Clarke | c Flintoff b SP Jones | 7 | (7) | b SP Jones | 39 |
| JN Gillespie | lbw b SP Jones | 26 | (8) | lbw b Hoggard | 0 |
| B Lee | c Trescothick b SP Jones | 1 | | not out | 18 |
| GD McGrath | not out | 1 | | not out | 5 |
| Extras | (b 8, lb 7, w 8, nb 15) | 38 | | (b 5, lb 8, w 1, nb 20) | 34 |
| Total | (84.5 overs) | 302 | | (for 9 wkts) (108 overs) | 371 |

| AUSTRALIA | O | M | R | W | | O | M | R | W |
|---|---|---|---|---|---|---|---|---|---|
| McGrath | 25 | 6 | 86 | 0 | | 20.5 | 1 | 115 | 5 |
| Lee | 27 | 6 | 100 | 4 | | 12 | 0 | 60 | 1 |
| Gillespie | 19 | 2 | 114 | 1 | (4) | 4 | 0 | 23 | 0 |
| Warne | 33.2 | 5 | 99 | 4 | (3) | 25 | 3 | 74 | 0 |
| Katich | 9 | 1 | 36 | 1 | | | | | |

| ENGLAND | O | M | R | W | | O | M | R | W |
|---|---|---|---|---|---|---|---|---|---|
| Harmison | 10 | 0 | 47 | 0 | | 22 | 4 | 67 | 2 |
| Hoggard | 6 | 2 | 22 | 0 | | 13 | 0 | 49 | 2 |
| Flintoff | 20 | 1 | 65 | 1 | (5) | 25 | 6 | 71 | 4 |
| SP Jones | 17.5 | 6 | 53 | 6 | (6) | 17 | 3 | 57 | 1 |
| Giles | 31 | 4 | 100 | 3 | (3) | 26 | 4 | 93 | 0 |
| Vaughan | | | | | (4) | 5 | 0 | 21 | 0 |

Fall of wickets:

| | Eng | Aus | Eng | Aus |
|---|---|---|---|---|
| 1st | 26 | 58 | 64 | 25 |
| 2nd | 163 | 73 | 97 | 96 |
| 3rd | 290 | 86 | 224 | 129 |
| 4th | 333 | 119 | 225 | 165 |
| 5th | 341 | 133 | 248 | 182 |
| 6th | 346 | 186 | 264 | 263 |
| 7th | 433 | 201 | – | 264 |
| 8th | 434 | 287 | – | 340 |
| 9th | 438 | 293 | – | 354 |
| 10th | 444 | 302 | – | – |

Close of play:
Day 1: Eng (1) 341–5 (Bell 59*, 89 overs)
Day 2: Aus (1) 214–7 (Warne 45*, Gillespie 4*, 56 overs)
Day 3: Aus (1) 264–7 (Warne 78*, Gillespie 7*, 70 overs)
Day 4: Aus (2) 24–0 (Langer 14*, Hayden 5*, 10 overs)

Man of the Match: RT Ponting
**Result:** **Match drawn**

and his team – just drinking and laughing about the old days. People who knew me, people who'd been tough on me, people who'd cared for me. I suppose it was like that Bruce Springsteen song 'Glory Days', only the other way around. I wasn't harking back to the days when I felt like a star. I was reconnecting with a more innocent time in my life. I wanted to stay there as long as I could, in a place where I belonged, surrounded by things that had meaning in my life.

I know it can't always be like that. Life is more complicated than that. You come from somewhere, but you have to make your own way. There are ties that bind, but you also need to break free. Life is a constant tension between belonging and leaving, saying goodbye and coming home – and when you do come back you are a different man and yet the same man.

Every now and then, for the odd magical moment, life feels joined up again. Your past and your present come together. You've reminded yourself who you are. People, places, events – everything in sync. Those times don't come around that often. The groundsman's hut, Old Trafford, 15 August 2005, was one of those moments.

As this is being written, ten years on, Pete Marron has recently died from cancer. I saw him in hospital on the day he died. Neil Fairbrother rang me just before:

'Pete has had his operation but now he's got an infection. You'd better go and see him.' He was on a ventilator. It was awful. I am glad I was in constant contact with him at the end. A great man who played a big role in my life.

All through the Ashes, I tried to escape between matches. After Old Trafford, a gang of us decamped to the South of France, near St-Tropez, and sat by the pool all week.

Getting there was a bit of a circus. Checking in my bags at the airport, I heard a familiar voice saying, 'All right, Freddie boy?'

It was David English. David runs the Bunbury cricket festival, so he'd known me since I was fourteen.

'What are you doing?' I asked him.

'Coming to France with you, Freddie.'

'Are you? OK.'

When we got to Nice airport, it was the usual high-summer constant traffic jam. Faced with a two- or three-hour drive down to St-Tropez, David says, 'I've got an idea, I'll sort this.'

I found him at the hire-company desk announcing, 'Come over here, Fred. I've got this helicopter.'

Then there was that moment when the bill is printed

off. And David hasn't moved. No gesture to the wallet. Not the merest suggestion of any hand movement in the direction of his wallet.

'Oh,' I eventually said. 'OK, Dave. Yeah, let me get this.' It was £500. Bloody hell.

But it was a great week, only temporarily ruined by leaving the villa at the top of the hill and venturing into St-Tropez town itself. Big mistake. Terrible place. Who do they think they are, these people? Sat on the back of a boat, an overpriced floating caravan. I felt like shouting at them, 'Why don't you move off that little floating table? There's a big world out there.' It's the worst place I've ever been. Not a real place at all.

When it was my turn to organise a meal for a big crowd of us we booked this fancy restaurant. The sushi comes out, then magnums of rosé. The bill? Ridiculous. Not somewhere I'll rush back to. Then an EasyJet flight back home and off to Nottingham for the fourth Test.


It was another classic match, which we won to take a 2–1 lead. I got a hundred in the first innings. It was all flowing for me now. Something had clicked into place. I wasn't seeing big fielders waiting to catch me. I was seeing boundaries, shots, sixes.

I had finally got the sound right in the dressing room, too. I was sick of the dreadful bomp-bomp-bomp nonsense music that some of the lads played. I swapped it for Elton John's 'Rocket Man'. I'm a big Elton fan. I'd met him in 2002 in Cape Town at a dinner with Desmond Tutu – I am pretty sure this did happen and I haven't just imagined it – one of the more bizarre and brilliant nights of my life. So the music was sorted. 'Rocket Man' became our anthem for that summer.

The night after my hundred at Trent Bridge, we all got together in the hotel bar – me and Rachael, Mum and Dad, Harmy. We moved on to the Living Room bar in town. Got kicked out eventually. I was wearing these baggy trousers that were all the rage at the time. Bit too big, to be honest, and they kept slipping down to my ankles. After a while, I just left them. The staff kept asking me to leave. Third time around, I thought, 'They're probably right. Time to go home.'

At that stage of my career I felt strong enough to bowl the next day in just about any condition. Especially in 2005. The crowd support gave you a false energy, as if you were superhuman. There is a particular kind of crowd that is in a state of genuine frenzied euphoria. Sometimes crowd noise can be whipped up for a short while by music and hype – but the deep excitement isn't

# England v Australia (4th Test)

*Played at Trent Bridge, Nottingham, on 25–28 August 2005*

Umpires: Aleem Dar & SA Bucknor (TV: MR Benson)
Referee: RS Madugalle
Toss: England

## ENGLAND

| | | | | | |
|---|---|---|---|---|---|
| ME Trescothick | b Tait | 65 | c Ponting b Warne | | 27 |
| AJ Strauss | c Hayden b Warne | 35 | c Clarke b Warne | | 23 |
| MP Vaughan* | c Gilchrist b Ponting | 58 | c Hayden b Warne | | 0 |
| IR Bell | c Gilchrist b Tait | 3 | c Kasprowicz b Lee | | 3 |
| KP Pietersen | c Gilchrist b Lee | 45 | c Gilchrist b Lee | | 23 |
| A Flintoff | lbw b Tait | 102 | b Lee | | 26 |
| GO Jones† | c and b Kasprowicz | 85 | c Kasprowicz b Warne | | 3 |
| AF Giles | lbw b Warne | 15 | not out | | 7 |
| MJ Hoggard | c Gilchrist b Warne | 10 | not out | | 8 |
| SJ Harmison | st Gilchrist b Warne | 2 | | | |
| SP Jones | not out | 15 | | | |
| Extras | (b 1, lb 15, w 1, nb 25) | 42 | (lb 4, nb 5) | | 9 |
| **Total** | (123.1 overs) | **477** | (for 7 wkts) (31.5 overs) | | **129** |

## AUSTRALIA

| | | | | | |
|---|---|---|---|---|---|
| JL Langer | c Bell b Hoggard | 27 | c Bell b Giles | | 61 |
| ML Hayden | lbw b Hoggard | 7 | c Giles b Flintoff | | 26 |
| RT Ponting* | lbw b SP Jones | 1 | run out (sub – GJ Pratt) | | 48 |
| DR Martyn | lbw b Hoggard | 1 | c GO Jones b Flintoff | | 13 |
| MJ Clarke | lbw b Harmison | 36 | c GO Jones b Hoggard | | 56 |
| SM Katich | c Strauss b SP Jones | 45 | lbw b Harmison | | 59 |
| AC Gilchrist† | c Strauss b Flintoff | 27 | lbw b Hoggard | | 11 |
| SK Warne | c Bell b SP Jones | 0 | st GO Jones b Giles | | 45 |
| B Lee | c Bell b SP Jones | 47 | not out | | 26 |
| MS Kasprowicz | b SP Jones | 5 | c GO Jones b Harmison | | 19 |
| SW Tait | not out | 3 | b Harmison | | 4 |
| Extras | (lb 2, w 1, nb 16) | 19 | (b 1, lb 4, nb 14) | | 19 |
| **Total** | (49.1 overs) | **218** | (124 overs) | | **387** |

| AUSTRALIA | O | M | R | W | | O | M | R | W |
|---|---|---|---|---|---|---|---|---|---|
| Lee | 32 | 2 | 131 | 1 | | 12 | 0 | 51 | 3 |
| Kasprowicz | 32 | 3 | 122 | 1 | | 2 | 0 | 19 | 0 |
| Tait | 24 | 4 | 97 | 3 | (4) | 4 | 0 | 24 | 0 |
| Warne | 29.1 | 4 | 102 | 4 | (3) | 13.5 | 2 | 31 | 4 |
| Ponting | 6 | 2 | 9 | 1 | | | | | |

| ENGLAND | O | M | R | W | | O | M | R | W |
|---|---|---|---|---|---|---|---|---|---|
| Harmison | 9 | 1 | 48 | 1 | (3) | 30 | 5 | 93 | 3 |
| Hoggard | 15 | 3 | 70 | 3 | (1) | 27 | 7 | 72 | 2 |
| SP Jones | 14.1 | 4 | 44 | 5 | (2) | 4 | 0 | 15 | 0 |
| Flintoff | 11 | 1 | 54 | 1 | | 29 | 4 | 83 | 2 |
| Giles | | | | | | 28 | 3 | 107 | 2 |
| Bell | | | | | | 6 | 2 | 12 | 0 |

Fall of wickets:

| | Eng | Aus | Aus | Eng |
|---|---|---|---|---|
| 1st | 105 | 20 | 50 | 32 |
| 2nd | 137 | 21 | 129 | 36 |
| 3rd | 146 | 22 | 155 | 57 |
| 4th | 213 | 58 | 161 | 57 |
| 5th | 241 | 99 | 261 | 103 |
| 6th | 418 | 157 | 277 | 111 |
| 7th | 450 | 157 | 314 | 116 |
| 8th | 450 | 163 | 342 | – |
| 9th | 454 | 175 | 373 | – |
| 10th | 477 | 218 | 387 | – |

Close of play: Day 1: Eng (1) 229–4 (Pietersen 33*, Flintoff 8*, 60 overs)
Day 2: Aus (1) 99–5 (Katich 20*, 30.3 overs)
Day 3: Aus (2) 222–4 (Clarke 39*, Katich 24*, 67 overs)

Man of the Match: A Flintoff
**Result:** **England won by 3 wickets**

there, it's not driving the pulse of the whole crowd. Then there's the real thing, when the crowd is so into the game that they've almost lost control. In 2005 it was like that all the way through the series.

I remember when we were trying to force a win at Old Trafford. I was bowling and I was just knackered. But I still managed to send them down at a good pace. I'd turn at the top of my mark and everyone was on their feet, just roaring at everything, driving me on.

By the fifth Test at The Oval, the whole country was at fever pitch. Though we made 373 in the first innings (I got 72), by the third evening we were in a bit of trouble. They were 277–2 and we were facing the prospect of a major first-innings deficit. That evening we'd arranged to have dinner at The Ivy – me and Rachael, Neil Fairbrother and his missus. I'd bowled plenty of overs that day, so the red wine went down particularly well. We had a few bottles and a very nice evening.

The next morning I was struggling a touch – a bit sore from bowling, a little dusty from the red wine. But I had this thing in my head that I wanted the Aussies to see me everywhere, to keep bumping into me. So I got into the ground uncharacteristically early on day four – I was first there – just to be around, certainly not to do extra practice.

You can smoke at the back of the Oval dressing rooms, so I had a fag right outside the Aussie rooms, welcoming them into the ground, almost one by one. I didn't really know any of them, but I did it anyway.

'Oh, morning, Ricky! Oh, Matthew, nice to see you, you all right?'

I finished my fag and got changed in the England dressing room, then arranged my coffee and fags right in front of the dressing room overlooking the pitch. I sat on the front there, having a second fag as the Aussies were going out to warm up.

'Morning, fellas. You all right? Morning, Shane!'

They were looking at me as if I was a bit odd, to be honest.

Now, I have a confession to make. I hate warm-ups with a passion. Worst part of the whole day. Nonsense, they are. Especially as I cherished forty-five minutes of quiet time before the actual start of play (coffee or tea, sandwich, cigarette). Some players like to practise right up to the start of play. But for me, whatever warming up I did was only going to be followed by cooling down again.

Duncan Fletcher once filmed me playing a stupid team warm-up game called 'Vortex', involving a kind of American football that whistles as it flies. It's supposed to make us all run around and 'wake up the competitive juices'. On Fletcher's video I 'warmed up' in an area about as wide as a dustbin lid. He said, 'Talk me through it.' My reply: 'I'm here to play cricket, not ------- Vortex.' We fell out about that.

It was another Vortex day on day four at The Oval, and all I wanted to do was bowl a few and get back into the dressing room. Out of the corner of my eye, I saw the Aussies doing just that, with McGrath, Lee and Tait on the square bowling into Gilchrist's gloves.

So I detached myself from the England group, picked a ball up and walked over to the Aussies.

'It's dragging on a bit over there,' I said to McGrath. 'I just want to bowl a couple, Glenn. Mind if I join in for a bit?'

And he just looks and says, 'What?'

'You don't mind, do you? Can I just bowl with you?'

Finally he says, 'Yeah.'

So the Aussies all had to take a break from their own practice while I marked out my run, pacing out the distance. When I ran in to bowl at Gilchrist, I was like the Tin Man, my body was so tight. But somehow I managed to hurl one at a decent clip and Gilchrist took it chest-high and threw it back to me.

I just rolled the ball back to him and said, 'Cheers, Adam. I'm good. Thanks very much, see you in a bit.'

As I walked off, McGrath stopped me and said, 'Fred, don't you get stiff?'

I replied, 'I don't know what you mean, Glenn.'

So much for the Freddie front. In reality, I walked into the dressing room like a cardboard cut-out, I was so stiff. I was also hung-over and five cigarettes down already. So I just sat in my spot for about an hour before play, taking my painkillers. Then we went out and I took a five-for and we bowled them out.

All through that summer, being out there in the middle was the best place to be. The worst place was sitting in the dressing room after you'd got out – looking on, powerless, just another onlooker. And the most excruciating example of that was in the second innings at The Oval.

We were, of course, trying to bat out the final day to win the Ashes for the first time in eighteen years. I'd hit Warne for six over his head and then he bowled the same ball. I should have just gone again. But I pulled out and, stuck in two minds, got caught-and-bowled.

I walked off thinking, 'I've lost it here. We've lost.' When I got back in the dressing room it wasn't like the normal anger, it was more of a numbness, a pure emptiness.

Kevin batted superbly for his 158 that day. But, well as he played, I'll be honest: it was just the worst innings to watch from the dressing room! The quicker Brett Lee bowled, the quicker Kevin's beans were going. He kept on swinging – whacking pulls, top-edging sixes, walking down and chatting as if he'd intended it all along. And the rest of us were just thinking, 'Oh, my word!'

As we sat there, we were counting down the overs, trying to work out how many Australia could chase if we were all out. Not that I'm much use in those situations. The hours of play, rules and regulations, overs in the last hour – not really my speciality. I have difficulty remembering how many overs there are in a day's play!

Ashley Giles's innings was also intriguing. As a cricketer, he was always a bit of an enigma to me. He was absolutely crucial to our success because he could bowl long, accurate spells. However, and I'm sure he won't mind me saying this, he's quite nervy as a bowler and as a person. He constantly needed assurance and building up. And yet he played some really important, high-pressure innings for us. Sometimes when he was batting – even though he was a number eight – he looked fully in control in a way that he didn't always seem to be as a bowler.

Strange to say, but at that moment during the fraught final day at The Oval – when everything was on the line, all we'd fought and played for – I had more confidence in Ashley hanging in there than in Kevin. I couldn't quell the fear that Kevin was about to get caught on the boundary. But he just kept going. And once he'd reached about 120, the pressure was released. We knew we'd be all right.

When we went out for those few overs in the field, with the match safe and the Ashes regained, Harmy bowled at the speed of light. He was so pumped up, he was flying in and the ball was rearing through to the keeper.

Standing at slip, I looked around the field, studying my England team-mates. Everyone was running on the spot or jumping in the air. It was really strange. It was like your body was full of this force and you couldn't get it out. In some ways it was like nerves, because when you get nervous you can't stop moving. But we weren't nervous any longer; we'd won the series.

Nervous with joy? Is that possible? I don't know. Maybe that's what total joy or ecstasy feels like: jumping around like an idiot.

\* \* \*

# England v Australia (5th Test)

*Played at The Oval, London, on 8–12 September 2005*

Umpires: BF Bowden & RE Koertzen (TV: JW Lloyds)
Referee:  RS Madugalle
Toss:     England

## ENGLAND

| | | | | | |
|---|---|---|---|---|---|
| ME Trescothick | c Hayden b Warne | 43 | lbw b Warne | | 33 |
| AJ Strauss | c Katich b Warne | 129 | c Katich b Warne | | 1 |
| MP Vaughan* | c Clarke b Warne | 11 | c Gilchrist b McGrath | | 45 |
| IR Bell | lbw b Warne | 0 | c Warne b McGrath | | 0 |
| KP Pietersen | b Warne | 14 | b McGrath | | 158 |
| A Flintoff | c Warne b McGrath | 72 | c and b Warne | | 8 |
| PD Collingwood | lbw b Tait | 7 | c Ponting b Warne | | 10 |
| GO Jones† | b Lee | 25 | b Tait | | 1 |
| AF Giles | lbw b Warne | 32 | b Warne | | 59 |
| MJ Hoggard | c Martyn b McGrath | 2 | not out | | 4 |
| SJ Harmison | not out | 20 | c Hayden b Warne | | 0 |
| Extras | (b 4, lb 6, w 1, nb 7) | 18 | (b 4, w 7, nb 5) | | 16 |
| **Total** | (105.3 overs) | **373** | (91.3 overs) | | **335** |

## AUSTRALIA

| | | | | |
|---|---|---|---|---|
| JL Langer | b Harmison | 105 | not out | 0 |
| ML Hayden | lbw b Flintoff | 138 | not out | 0 |
| RT Ponting* | c Strauss b Flintoff | 35 | | |
| DR Martyn | c Collingwood b Flintoff | 10 | | |
| MJ Clarke | lbw b Hoggard | 25 | | |
| SM Katich | lbw b Flintoff | 1 | | |
| AC Gilchrist† | lbw b Hoggard | 23 | | |
| SK Warne | c Vaughan b Flintoff | 0 | | |
| B Lee | c Giles b Hoggard | 6 | | |
| GD McGrath | c Strauss b Hoggard | 0 | | |
| SW Tait | not out | 1 | | |
| Extras | (b 4, lb 8, w 2, nb 9) | 23 | (lb 4) | 4 |
| **Total** | (107.1 overs) | **367** | (for 0 wkts) (0.4 overs) | **4** |

| AUSTRALIA | O | M | R | W | | O | M | R | W |
|---|---|---|---|---|---|---|---|---|---|
| McGrath | 27 | 5 | 72 | 2 | | 26 | 3 | 85 | 3 |
| Lee | 23 | 3 | 94 | 1 | | 20 | 4 | 88 | 0 |
| Tait | 15 | 1 | 61 | 1 | (5) | 5 | 0 | 28 | 1 |
| Warne | 37.3 | 5 | 122 | 6 | (3) | 38.3 | 3 | 124 | 6 |
| Katich | 3 | 0 | 14 | 0 | | | | | |
| Clarke | | | | | (4) | 2 | 0 | 6 | 0 |

| ENGLAND | O | M | R | W | | O | M | R | W |
|---|---|---|---|---|---|---|---|---|---|
| Harmison | 22 | 2 | 87 | 1 | | 0.4 | 0 | 0 | 0 |
| Hoggard | 24.1 | 2 | 97 | 4 | | | | | |
| Flintoff | 34 | 10 | 78 | 5 | | | | | |
| Giles | 23 | 1 | 76 | 0 | | | | | |
| Collingwood | 4 | 0 | 17 | 0 | | | | | |

Fall of wickets:

| | Eng | Aus | Eng | Aus |
|---|---|---|---|---|
| 1st | 82 | 185 | 2 | – |
| 2nd | 102 | 264 | 67 | – |
| 3rd | 104 | 281 | 67 | – |
| 4th | 131 | 323 | 109 | – |
| 5th | 274 | 329 | 126 | – |
| 6th | 289 | 356 | 186 | – |
| 7th | 297 | 359 | 199 | – |
| 8th | 325 | 363 | 308 | – |
| 9th | 345 | 363 | 335 | – |
| 10th | 373 | 367 | 335 | – |

Close of play:  Day 1: Eng (1) 319–7 (Jones 21*, Giles 5*, 88 overs)
Day 2: Aus (1) 112–0 (Langer 75*, Hayden 32*, 33 overs)
Day 3: Aus (1) 277–2 (Hayden 110*, Martyn 9*, 78.4 overs)
Day 4: Eng (2) 34–1 (Trescothick 14*, Vaughan 19*, 13.2 overs)

Man of the Match: KP Pietersen
**Result:**          **Match drawn**

I found the post-game stuff odd, though. In my interview with Michael Atherton during the presentation ceremony, people told me it looked like I just wanted to get off the stage. Needing attention in one way, yet hating attention when it comes. A familiar story.

It's strange, when I look back on that series and that summer. I don't have too many strong recollections of actually being on the field. I can see little flashes of what happened when I was out there, but I don't remember it that well.

But I do remember sitting with Harmy in the dressing room, having a beer after we'd won the Ashes. We were excited, of course we were. But we were also a little confused. We'd done this together, two great friends. But how? Two lads, one from a rough spot in the north-east, one from a tough corner of Preston, neither of us destined to play cricket – how had it all happened?

We talked it through, in our little corner of the dressing room. The significance of the occasion was only just beginning to dawn on us – even though the sport was all over. For much of the series, I'd been semi-deliberately oblivious to everything apart from just playing. That's why I'd kept going away. At long last, in that conversation, we began to see what it meant – to the crowd, to the country; how we'd been part of something special and rare. It wasn't just another series. It was something much more. Harmy was the perfect person to share it with. If Keysey could have been there too, that would have been the icing on the cake. It was an amazing moment.

The nature of the TV coverage had played a massive part. Because it was broadcast on Channel 4 rather than Sky Sports, every match was free and available for everyone to watch. The series shaped and defined the English summer. It's not my intention to get into a debate over the pros and cons of satellite TV – I can see that Sky fund English cricket to a large degree. There are arguments both ways. But some things are undeniable. The fact that millions of people were able to watch the Ashes that summer was a central factor in making it so intense and memorable.

Looking back on that series, though the competition was fierce at the time, I realise I was lucky to play against a great Australian side. I had the opportunity to compete with the likes of Ponting, Gilchrist, Warne and McGrath. And you're judged by the way you play against the Aussies, just as, back in the 1980s, it was how you played against the West Indies, because they were the side to beat then. If I'd been playing just any old team, the public wouldn't have cared as much as they did. So I have a kind of love–hate relationship with Australia to this day. I still work out there in the winters, the foe they've almost come to accept. It's played a big part in my life.

One feature of the series was how often I dismissed Adam Gilchrist (four times). Of course it's tempting to talk about planning and preparation and team meetings spent poring over technical glitches and flaws. But it wouldn't be true.

I spoke to Adam about it recently when I wrote the foreword to his book. He wanted to understand how I'd arrived at the 'plan' of coming around the wicket to him, which led to my success.

'I don't know what you mean,' I said.

'Well, why did you did formulate that idea?' Adam insisted.

'I didn't. I just bowl quicker round the wicket. That was the only reason I came round the wicket to you. You missed a couple. And then I just kept doing it.'

Adam thought there must have been some great master plan. Far from it. I just complete my action better bowling round the wicket.

Let me say something I've been wanting to say for years about plans and team meetings. For 99 per cent of batsmen, a bowler's plans do not change. I can think of one and that's about it. Bowling at Mohammad Yousuf, it was always worth trying to knock him over first ball with a full, straight one. And very occasionally, you sense that someone doesn't fancy the short ball.

Everyone else? Top of off. It really is that simple. Just bowl it there. It's what batsmen don't like. So it makes me laugh when people say, 'Oh, he's good off his legs.' Who isn't good off his legs? No one. And who doesn't like short and wide? No one. All you learnt from those meetings was that the better the opposition batsmen, the longer we spent going round and round in circles.

A cricket team would be well served by having a one-minute meeting at the start of every season. The captain should say, 'Unless anyone can think of a compelling reason otherwise, let's assume we are trying to bowl at the top of off-stump, shall we? Great, now let's talk about something interesting.'

For me, visualisation was always infinitely more useful than those meetings, which sometimes seemed to be nothing more than a form of job justification. That summer, I had come to realise that there was a way of practising without straining your body or getting injured. (If I was lukewarm at best about practising batting, I actively disliked bowling in the nets. It hurts too much!) Instead of literal practice, I used to play the contest through in my head. If I was driving home or just sitting around, I'd often be bowling in my head.

Let me try to explain how it worked. Imagine driving a car, but instead of looking out at the road and steering, you are controlling everything by looking at a small screen. On that 'screen' in my head, I would be very precise about the way I played cricket. I used to reach my mark and very consciously stop, then I'd put the ball in my hand, clear my mind by looking down for a second and at that point decide where I was going to bowl. I'd be looking forward, but not looking *at* anything in particular. Just looking into the distance. There was never a specific batter involved. There was *someone* batting on the screen, but I couldn't tell you who it was, because I wouldn't have a mental picture of him. And then I'd run and bowl. It was all in my head, but it felt totally real.

I became confident that it made me ready for the contest. After all, I didn't change too much from ball to ball. It was a bit different in ODIs, but in Tests I kept things very simple. People often forget that as a bowler everything's in your hands. The batsman has to react to what you've done. Batting's reactive; he's got to make a decision once it's come out of your hand. As a bowler, all you can do is land the ball where you want to. That's it. Yes, you're on your own. But if you can master your mind, there shouldn't be too much that can mess you around.

I used to almost trick myself into thinking I'd done things before, because I'd rehearsed them so many times in my head. When I picked up the ball and wanted to do something, in my mind the feeling that I'd done it before was so strong that I actually believed I had. That's stayed with me ever since. Even now, when I'm performing on stage, I feel I've done things before – even as I'm doing them for the first time.

That open-top bus ride around London? I was struggling. I do have flashbacks. We got on the bus and they gave us champagne and it was like, 'Why are you giving us champagne? We've had enough.' And ask anyone – where's the best place to send a bunch of drunken blokes? To a garden party at 10 Downing Street, of course.

As a kid I liked *Through the Keyhole*, so here was a great chance to have a nose around. I found my way to the Cabinet Room. I thought I knew which seat the Prime Minister sits in, so I took that one, then I put my feet on the table. I had a bottle of beer in my hand and I started hosting my own meeting. I was the only man in the room, but I began talking to the Home Secretary and the Chancellor.

Then a security guard abruptly called the meeting to a close by kicking me out and marching me back to join the rest of the group.

# 6

# CAPTAINS AND COACHES

I f I was up, I could bring the dressing room up. If I was down, I could bring the dressing room down. Looking back, I can see how I might affect a dressing room more than some players do. But you're not going to be up all the time; that's just human nature. In fact, I think I may have needed more help than some players do. That's part of your job as a coach, understanding players, helping them through the bad times. Yes, I was hard work at times. But if a coach gave me a little bit, I'd give it back tenfold.

With Duncan Fletcher, the man who was in charge for the majority of my time in an England sweater, I got off to a bad start. Even I can't say that was his fault. In 1999, Duncan had been appointed as the next England coach but he continued to manage Glamorgan until the end of his contract. So for the summer of 1999 he was England's coach elect. When I was introduced to Duncan, I was lying on a hotel floor in Blackpool, during the Lancashire v Glamorgan game. I'd been out drinking with Matthew Maynard, the Glamorgan captain (my part in the game was over, if that's any excuse). Their physio walked through the hotel with Duncan and said, as he passed me, 'Duncan, that's your future all-rounder.' 'Nice to meet you,' I replied from the vantage point of the hotel carpet. I think Duncan saw the funny side and it wasn't a big deal. It was certainly an unusual way to be formally introduced.

As England coach, Duncan did some really good things for the side. He helped us to start winning again. The main issue with Duncan, for me, however, was the question of favouritism. The frustrating thing was there were some people in the dressing room he wouldn't even speak to. There were others he couldn't do enough for.

I've never been – and never will be – someone who 'plays the game' with people. I don't suck up to anyone or do any of that. I point-blank refuse. I just hate it. Instinctively, I always sided with the new players or the unfashionable ones, because when you went into the side at first it could feel like you were an outcast. My thinking was 'Nobody should come into this dressing room like that; it's just wrong.'

I always wanted to get to know new players coming

into the team. One, I genuinely find people interesting. Much as I enjoy going to places and having new adventures, I enjoy meeting people even more. Two, for a team to be successful it's important to make everyone feel part of it straight away. Otherwise, you're playing with only nine or ten.

I think it's a key part of the coach's job to make the team feel as good as they possibly can, every time they walk out. But the other players share that duty. There were times when we spent a lot of time talking about the opposition, but not so much about what made our own players tick. Never mind the opposition – it's much more important that your mate feels good about what he's doing, and that you can recognise the signals if he's not.

Sometimes, however, it seemed that my friendships with new players lasted only until they felt able to move onwards and upwards. I remember when Paul Collingwood first came into the dressing room, we did everything together. We practised together, trained together, had dinner together; we batted together and did well in games together – we were thick as thieves. When he got established, he just binned me. Maybe I did something to upset him, but it seemed to me he positioned himself where he felt he needed to be.

I think that was partly to do with the culture Duncan

created – there were 'ins' and 'outs', favourites and outcasts, people he wanted and people he could barely tolerate.

There is certainly an alternative view on Duncan. If you speak to Marcus Trescothick, he will tell you that Duncan did a huge amount for him. Marcus was a good player as a kid, but through Duncan's influence he became the best batsman I ever played with. Hussain and Collingwood also rated Duncan very highly. It was only a select few. And the frustration was that if he could do that with some people, why didn't he help everyone?

My relationship with Duncan was weird. At times, he spoke to me a lot and things were fine. When I took five wickets at Barbados, he was there at the side waving. And he was genuinely really happy for me. He was the same in India in 2006 when we won the Test in Mumbai, even though we'd had some issues on that tour. I picked him up during the celebrations.

I understand that my performances couldn't be like that all the time. But if Duncan could have shown me more of that side, I would have given more back. At times, I wanted to believe we were developing a better relationship. Then within five minutes he'd take it all away.

special feeling: with my family after my final Test match.

Keeping wicket with Chris in the back garden, aged six.

Pondering my next move, aged nine.

Splashing about with my parents.

At Old Trafford, so central to my cricket, and wearing my Lancashire sweater.

o central figures in my early days at
ncashire, Mike Watkinson and Neil
rbrother.

The wonderfully gifted Ben Hollioake
shaking hands with England U19s coach
John Abrahams.

hat happiness looks like: lifting the NatWest Trophy at Lord's with Lancashire
1998.

I owe so much to the late Pete Marron: groundsman, landlord and Lancashire legend.

Freeing my arms against West Indies.

I was proud to meet the Queen during the Test match against West Indies at Lord's in 2004.

...e first ball in the opening Test of the 2005 Ashes. The atmosphere in the Long
...om said it all.

...knowledging the crowd after
...oring 73 in the 'greatest Test' against
...stralia at Edgbaston in 2005.

With Brett Lee at Edgbaston: only a few
words were said, but the photo captures the
moment.

The culmination of an exciting phase in English cricket, winning the Ashes in 2005.

Walking with the man who so often got me fit and motivated, Dave 'Rooster' Robert

mething about Alastair Cook impressed me from day one. I was determined that was selected in his triumphant debut Test.

th Liam Plunkett: as you would expect, two northern fast bowlers relaxing over a ne of chess,

Downcast after net practice in 2007. Over time I found visualisation was just as important as actual practice.

This photo shows the inevitable strai bowling puts on your body.

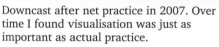

An unlikely but crucial dismissal, my run-out of Ricky Ponting in the final day of th 2009 Ashes.

Sometimes he scarcely spoke to me at all. I saw him do it with other people as well. Duncan didn't really have much of an impact on my game (though I did know I had to play really well to stay in the side). And, as a person, I don't know Duncan any better now than when I started playing under him.

One contribution he did make was messing up the way I played spin. Up till then I would simply stay still and then try to hit it. And I had always done all right against spin. Then I had a bad patch and Duncan got me doing his 'forward press' technique, and that completely ruined me. Doubtless Duncan had only good intentions about trying to improve my game against spin. But he could be one-eyed with his coaching ideas – it was his way or else he wasn't interested. Troy Cooley, the bowling coach, had mastered a more flexible approach. He was different with all of us fast bowlers. His real skill was knowing what to say to which player.

When I started getting injured, that's when the real problems with Duncan began. I'd struggled with hernias and all sorts of physical problems. Perhaps he didn't believe I was injured. He seemed to take it as a personal attack on him that I couldn't play.

It was as though Duncan was worried about any blame landing at his door. He is a clever man and he always gave the impression of having a strategy for every situation. Maybe that's why I found Duncan very awkward to be around. And playing cricket is hard enough without worrying about the mood of the coach.

Duncan had undoubted gifts. One thing I found hard to forgive, however, was his apparent desire to humiliate the people he disliked. For some reason, he took strongly against Monty Panesar. Very, very strongly. How can you dislike Monty? He is not someone it is easy to dislike. Sure, he has his strengths and weaknesses as a cricketer – he could bowl, tried hard with the bat and was far from a natural fielder – but humiliating him? Hard to understand.

One game, when I was captain for an ODI, Fletcher told me that Panesar was likely to be in the World Cup squad. I said, 'All right, good.'

Next, Duncan asked me where I was going to field him in the following day's ODI.

I said, I'd 'hide' him in a position where the ball didn't go too much – a standard thing that captains do with weaker fielders.

'No, put Monty at backward point,' Duncan shot back at me.

This was bizarre. Monty at backward point, usually the star fielder's position, really?

'Yeah, expose him,' Duncan explained. 'Show everyone how bad he is at fielding.'

'I don't think I can do that, Duncan,' I said. 'Monty can field at "forty-five" [a relatively easy place to field, like a short fine leg] and if he stops it, good on him.'

It seemed to me that Duncan wanted me to expose Monty because he didn't want him out on the pitch. Having failed to win a disagreement with the selectors, he was trying to use his influence in other areas to win the argument. Humiliating Monty was all part of the plan. It wasn't a plan I could buy into.

That incident was revealing. In the preceding months, I'd been captain during the 2006–07 Ashes disaster. I was certainly to blame for a lot of it. Of course I was – I was the captain. But Duncan neatly detached himself. He made sure that I was isolated and, just as importantly, that I looked isolated. I was like a dead man walking.

At the end of that long, bleak winter came the most infamous clash between Duncan and me, the 'Fredalo' incident. Again, I have no desire to wriggle out of any

91

blame. The aftermath, however, included some vintage Duncan manoeuvres. Looking back, I was treated to the full Duncan experience.

A bit of background. Around that time I was doing a lot of swimming for fitness and I'd become quite a strong swimmer. During that 2007 World Cup in the West Indies, I would routinely swim a couple of kilometres, out to a boat near the shore and then back again. This was during the day, I should point out, and I'd be sober! In St Lucia, I remember I swam up to a little boat and the family turned out to be English. They recognised me and asked me on board for a cup of tea. I had a brew with them, then swam back to the hotel.

Maybe all this was in the back of my mind, at some subliminal level, when I tried to get on board that pedalo. I'd never intended to go out after that New Zealand match. We'd been beaten and I'd got out first ball. But I had a couple of impromptu drinks with two umpires – I won't name them as they are very good men – and then my evening spiralled out of control.

We ended up in a bar with several players. And I got drunk. For some reason, I got this idea in my head about having a beer with Ian Botham, who was on a boat nearby. So as I sat on a bar stool with my head spinning, I began weighing up how to get there. (In fact, I had the wrong boat – turns out it was Tim Rice's boat I was aiming for, and he probably wouldn't have been best pleased if I'd managed the trip successfully.)

I left the bar and set out on my own. Initially, I had a crack with a kayak, but it didn't have a paddle, so I was struggling there. Then I tried with a pedalo and dragged it into the water, about knee-deep. But I just couldn't get on to it because I kept falling over. The waves would roll in and over I'd go.

Falling over, getting wet, struggling up again, being knocked down by the next wave. I began laughing, then it turned into a fit of laughter, uncontrollable. Partly it was the ridiculousness of the situation – on my own, splashing around helplessly with a small boat – and partly something much deeper. It was the first time I'd laughed – really laughed – in a long, long time.

So, on reflection, was it a good plan – when I could scarcely stand up – to try to climb on to a pedalo, then moored on a St Lucia beach, and pedal out to Tim Rice's boat? Certainly not. And yet in the state I was in, at that particular moment, in the context of my life at the time, for some reason that's obviously what I wanted to do. I'm sure there was one voice in my head saying, 'This isn't the best of ideas. You are in no state to swim. Don't do this.' But the other voice was stronger. And I'm still not sure it was the wrong thing to do, in the wider scheme of things. Sometimes I think you need to make a big mistake before you can start over again.

The next morning, I woke up in my hotel room on top of my bed, jeans and shirt still on. You know that moment, before you open your eyes, when you check how you're feeling and run through the events of the night before. And then you think, 'Oh no . . .'

There was a knock at the door. Usually it's the hotel cleaners or room service. So I said, 'Could you come back in a minute?' There was a second series of knocks. My replies were getting shorter now, as I kept asking them to come back later. Then a third loud knocking. I hauled myself up and peered through the slats in the wooden door, mumbling angrily, 'Will you please go . . . Oh, good morning, Duncan!'

I opened the door wearing the previous night's clothes, sand and wet footprints everywhere. I must have looked a sight.

'There is a hearing in my room – now,' Duncan announced.

\* \* \*

It was a strange meeting and I ended up getting upset. Even stranger was the full team meeting that came afterwards. Somehow the idea had been introduced that there was a team curfew. In truth, we had never had a team curfew, not once. But now there was supposed to have been a midnight curfew – applied retrospectively!

In the middle of the meeting room there was another flip chart, and on it were the initials of everyone in the squad. We had to get up one by one and write what time we had got back to the hotel after the night out.

The problem was, of course, that I had absolutely no idea. But, not wanting to appear to be hiding anything, I got up and wrote '3.30 a.m.' on the board. (I later discovered that I'd got in at 1.30, so I did myself out of two hours!) One of the lads – who'd been out later than anyone – conveniently said he'd made it back at ten minutes to twelve. Getting back after midnight meant the player got fined. That included a couple of lads who were just playing pool across the road, not even drinking. So I fought their corner. And, fortunately, they didn't have to pay the fine. Though I wonder if that estranged me even more from Duncan.

What had started out as a disciplinary meeting had turned into a political one. Some people seemed to know in advance the right things to say in order to keep on the right side of the management.

But the most bizarre incident during the 'Fredalo' saga happened just before the press conference, when Duncan spoke to me about my being banned for one match, against Canada, as it turned out.

Duncan was exaperated with me. I can understand that – I'd got in trouble once too often. But he said something to me that seemed so odd that I'll never forget it: 'What have you ever done for me?'

'I don't know what you mean, Duncan,' I replied, very surprised. 'What are you on about?'

'Well, one of the lads gets me Asics trainers, another one gets me Oakley sunglasses. What have *you* ever done for me?'

I was staggered. How had the conversation got on to a pair of trainers? I'm being banned by England and here we are talking about shoes?

Of course, later you think up a lot of clever replies that would have been funny at the time. 'Well, Duncan, I did play a hand in the 2005 Ashes.' Or 'Aren't you an OBE now, Duncan?' Instead, the thought in my head was 'But, Duncan, if only you'd told me your waist size and inside leg, I could have got you a pair of tracksuit trousers.'

The press conference continued in the same surreal

mode. The reporter from Sky News shouted out, 'Can you confirm there was a pedalo involved?' The country's sports media was interrogating me about my relations with a small plastic boat. There was something especially absurd about being asked a serious question on a ridiculous theme.

Then a journalist asked Duncan a question: if the next match had been against Australia rather than Canada, would I still have been banned?

Duncan's answer was full of ifs and buts, and the difficulty of hypotheticals, and on the one hand and yet on the other . . .

I very nearly shouted out, 'Just answer the question, Duncan. Just say you would have banned me. It's fine. Because if you *wouldn't* have banned me for a more high-profile match, then what is this all about?'


There was one peculiar meeting still to come – when Duncan announced he was retiring. He did it at a practice session. We were all brought into a circle and he told us the news. Vaughany spoke about Duncan and started welling up – fair enough, they'd had a long partnership. Could it be that I saw one of Fletcher's henchmen in the team stab himself in the leg trying to induce a few tears?

And when Paul Nixon looked like he might cry as well, I did think to myself, 'Hang on a minute, Nico, you've only played a handful of games.'

Me? I was looking around for someone to high-five. And when Peter Moores took over, for me it was a breath of fresh air. But given my relationship with Duncan by that time, if Idi Amin had taken over as coach, I'd still have been doing handstands.

One of the questions I ask myself about Duncan is how much was my fault. I've never been easy; I'm the first to admit that. And I was probably even more difficult to handle when I was a young cricketer. But when I go through all the captains and coaches I've played under, there aren't many I've really clashed with.

Johnny Abrahams was coach at England Under-19s – an amazing man who I went back to at the end of my career when I was trying to rediscover some freedom with the bat.

Mike Watkinson was my first captain at Lancashire and then became coach. He gave me my chance. We are very different sorts of people. But there was never much friction.

The Sri Lankan-born Australian Dav Whatmore coached Lancashire in the late 1990s. Dav copped me at my worst and I can understand that I never completely won him over.

As for captains, I loved playing under John Crawley. We had different styles as people and players – he was a classical batsman and Cambridge-educated. Watching him bat when he was on form was amazing. And he was superb at noticing little things that had crept into my game. John held his corner too, didn't back down if he felt he was justified. And he'd be the first to have fun in the dressing room over a pint and a fag.

Warren Hegg took over from John. Everyone liked Heggy, Lancashire legend. He tried to sell you shirts off the back of a lorry. But no one minded.

Mark Chilton was another public schoolboy turned Lancashire captain who was much tougher than he looked, a bit like Andrew Strauss that way. Chilly jumped up and gave me a whack on the chin one night when a drinking game got out of hand. I was pushing my luck as usual and he drew the line. Everyone played for Chilly and that's all you can ask.

Michael Vaughan really knew his players, as I mentioned earlier; knew how to adapt his methods for different individuals. He also had the ability to hide things well; he was unflappable and gave nothing away. That is a great strength. Setting funny fields was all part of the act. He loved being the maverick captain and the attention it brought.

I enjoyed playing with Andrew Strauss. With the captaincy, the way it worked out, we tended to captain in each other's absence. When I did play under him a little at the end of my career, he was his usual self – a good, solid lad. You can set your watch by him. Strauss himself has said he never claimed to be a tactical genius: 'It's not so much about making the right decision as making the decisions right.' By that he meant, I think, that the key to a lot of management is persuading people to buy into the decision. The decision itself might be a genuine fifty–fifty. It's what happens *after* the decision that matters.

That point is relevant to Kevin Pietersen's time as captain. He had real strengths. He set a fine example with his massive work ethic – fitness, practice, everything. You couldn't fault him there. Less well-known is that Kevin has a superb cricket brain. He is often absolutely spot on. When he bats, I think the whole game opens up before him. He reads games and situations really well. Reading people I think he finds much harder. I think he got frustrated. He found it frustrating that other people couldn't do the things he could do. Why couldn't they string six balls together as he wanted? Why couldn't they bat like him and make a score? What was so difficult about that? Well, it was hard for some people. I think losing the captaincy really affected Kevin over the long term. I don't think he was used to not succeeding at something. He saw it as a blot on his copybook. And he wasn't used to being told no. But then I don't think any of us are.

With new coach Peter Moores, I just hit it off straight away. You won't be surprised to hear that I managed to annoy him once, though. We were all enjoying a long night's drinking and talking at the house of an Indian sponsor and industrial magnate. I say house. It was more like a whole village. When the waiter asked what I wanted to drink, I said, 'I'll have a bottle of Dom Perignon 1996.' Just as a joke.

'No problem, sir,' he replied, not a flicker of surprise or concern.

We drank a whole case. Somewhere along the way, I said something negative about cricket to Mooresy.

He said, 'If I had a pound for every time you've used that phrase, I'd be a rich man.'

'If I had a pound for every time you've stood in that silly camp pose with your hand on your hip, I'd be even richer.'

It kicked off a bit, and Hugh Morris, managing director of England cricket, and Harmy stepped in to diffuse the whole thing. Next morning, I woke up with that sinking feeling again. 'Oh no, what have I done? I've alienated the coach. I like this fella. What did I do that for?'

First thing that morning, as I walked towards the team bus, Mooresy was standing by the door. He had this huge grin on his face. I smiled. He gave me a wink. I got on the bus. That was it. Done and dusted. Never mentioned again. That's Pete. No grudges, no politics, just does what he thinks is right, and does it with a smile.

Twice now he has built the foundation of a good England team. In 2008, he did it before Kevin forced him out. And recently, we've seen a lot of Peter's good work pay off with the new England team. Sadly for Peter, he got sacked before he received the credit he deserved. It was typically fair of Alastair Cook to pay tribute to Peter when England won the Ashes at Trent Bridge in 2015.

The captains and coaches who brought the best out of me not only challenged me, but also encouraged an element of fun. It was on an England 'A' tour to South Africa when I first played under Michael Vaughan. John Emburey was coach and my main feeling about the whole experience was 'Wow. Perfect. I'm being paid to go on holiday with my mates and play cricket.' On the strength of my form on that tour I was picked for the 1999 World Cup.

What does all this say about me and Duncan? I wasn't always the easiest. Hands up on that front. But I think I was unlucky that for most of my England career I had bad personal chemistry with the man in charge.

# 7

# PLAYING AGAINST MYSELF

WE have a rule in our household: you commit to things 100 per cent, have a proper go, or you don't get involved. No half-measures.

Throughout my career, inside cricket and also afterwards, I've engineered situations where I am committed to something. I like to put myself in for things I'm not sure I can do. That's Fred. That's one way I get my kicks. Right up until the last minute, I'm still not sure I can do it. But there aren't any exits.

What about the easy option of just bailing out? I've certainly thought about it. Once, in particular. There was definitely a period when a part of me wanted to escape the firing line. That was caused by the 5–0 Ashes defeat in 2006–07 when I was captain.

How would I have done that? Well, I could have used an injury to get out of the tour. I could have used my ankle as an excuse. But it would have been wrong and there's no way I could have gone through with it.

I started thinking about everything too much. As a batsman, trying to play the perfect shots. Thinking too much about captaincy, too. I was trying to live up to the 2005 thing, I was trying to get better, I was trying to lead a team, I was trying to juggle everything. It all got too much. So I'd go to my room and have a drink. That was probably the only time I felt comfortable, after a bottle. Then the next day I'd be embarrassed, thinking, 'Oh, I messed that up.'

Asking for help? I was really bad at that. The problem was who to ask. I spoke to Harmy quite openly, as Harmy had always spoken to me honestly. But he was fighting his own stuff. And when I looked at the coaching staff and team-mates, I saw self-preservation kicking in.

Did I make mistakes? Plenty. But I'm not sure how much 'choice' I had, from that point of view. It's hard to say I could have done things differently, because I probably couldn't have. You take the option that feels available to you at the time, not the path that looks good with the benefit of hindsight.

In difficult times, I think you resort to your default character. For me, when things went wrong, that meant escaping – through psychological isolation and through wine. It's a tendency I've still got to watch. I'm happy living with my own thoughts in my own head. But that doesn't lend itself ideally to a team sport (or family life, for that matter). In 2006–07 that tendency tripped into an outright problem. I was isolating myself not because I was comfortable with self-sufficiency but to avoid situations. I was embarrassed to see people because it was going so badly. I couldn't look people in the eye. I couldn't speak to people – team-mates, fans, family, everyone.

Just after that, following the disastrous 2007 World Cup, I thought about stopping playing cricket altogether. It was around the time that Duncan Fletcher's book was published. I didn't read it – I don't read many cricket books, so I definitely wasn't going to read Duncan's – but I knew it was all kicking off.

I was in America at the time. I was recovering from surgery again – up to about number six now – and driving up and down the M60 at 6 a.m. in cold weather to go to the gym hadn't really helped my mood, so to get into a different space we had decamped to Florida for some warm-weather training. We rented a house for three months at a golf resort in Palm Beach – a bit *Stepford*

*Wives*, but very nice. Nobody knew anything about me; nobody even knew who I was. I loved it.

At one point the exchange rate was about two dollars to the pound. I said to the missus, 'Shall we cash our chips now and just live here? We could open a café or something.' And we genuinely thought about it. The rental house had one CD, by Jack Johnson. We used to play it over and over and over. And my daughter would be jumping in the pool and my elder son was about eighteen months old. The song was 'Better Together'. It was the perfect title for how we felt at that time.

That scene wasn't real life, however. I knew that I'd have got fed up with Palm Beach eventually. It was nice, but it was a way of hiding or escaping. I detached myself completely. I didn't see anything, didn't read anything. I just got my head down in training and began to feel better again.

When we came back home, the doubts returned. Shortly after Peter Moores took over, I had a meeting with him at Loughborough. We sat down and I was completely honest. 'You know what?' I explained. 'I'm not sure if I want to carry on playing. I'm struggling fitness-wise, and in my head. In Australia I probably drank a little bit more than I should have. And now I'm not sure what I want to do.'

The beauty of the conversation was that Pete was almost like a stranger. Though I'd played a little against him, I didn't really know him. And it wasn't the kind of chat where he was telling me what to do. We just had a low-key conversation about it all. Pete mostly listened, but he also challenged me. How could the factors I was describing outweigh the prospect of playing for England again? Afterwards, I left the room feeling a lot better than when I went in. I felt brighter about the future.

Above all, it would have been the easy option to walk away. Strangely, that thought spurred me to do the opposite, to turn it around. So the whole experience – the whitewash, the captaincy, the shocking World Cup – ended up making me hungrier to play. I just wanted to get back out there and set it all straight. If my career had been all good, it would have been easy enough to say, 'I've had a good run and that'll do me.' But because everything had gone to pot for a while, I felt compelled to keep coming back.

The hardest thing at the end, in 2009, was that I beat myself. It was my body that let me down, couldn't take any more. By that stage, I felt I was playing against myself, which was more fun than playing any opposition.

It was the same old contest, seeing how far I could push myself until my body gave in. And it did eventually. Even now, I wonder whether I should have been able to get through it, should have carried on further.

The high point – if that's the right term – of that feeling of playing against myself was at Lord's, the second Ashes Test in 2009. They were only a moderate Australia team, but that was beside the point. The way I felt, the Australians were incidental.

On the final day we needed five wickets to win, Australia needed 200 runs. I took the wicket of Brad Haddin with the fourth ball. After that I spoke to Andrew Strauss, the captain: 'Just to let you know I'll keep bowling until all the wickets are gone.'

A bit later there was another chat, deep into my spell, when my knee was giving way. Stop bowling? I was pretty direct with Straussy: 'I'm going to bowl them out. Trying to take me off is going to get embarrassing because I'm going to walk back to my mark with the ball and you're somehow going to have to get it out of my hand. You'll have to send me off the field to get me to stop bowling.'

\* \* \*

# England v Australia (2nd Test)

*Played at Lord's Cricket Ground, London, on 16–20 July 2009*

Umpires:  BR Doctrove & RE Koertzen (TV: NJ Llong)
Referee:   JJ Crowe
Toss:       England

## ENGLAND

| | | | | | |
|---|---|---|---|---|---|
| AJ Strauss* | b Hilfenhaus | 161 | c Clarke b Hauritz | | 32 |
| AN Cook | lbw b Johnson | 95 | lbw b Hauritz | | 32 |
| RS Bopara | lbw b Hilfenhaus | 18 | c Katich b Hauritz | | 27 |
| KP Pietersen | c Haddin b Siddle | 32 | c Haddin b Siddle | | 44 |
| PD Collingwood | c Siddle b Clarke | 16 | c Haddin b Siddle | | 54 |
| MJ Prior† | b Johnson | 8 | run out (North) | | 61 |
| A Flintoff | c Ponting b Hilfenhaus | 4 | not out | | 30 |
| SCJ Broad | b Hilfenhaus | 16 | not out | | 0 |
| GP Swann | c Ponting b Siddle | 4 | | | |
| JM Anderson | c Hussey b Johnson | 29 | | | |
| G Onions | not out | 17 | | | |
| Extras | (b 15, lb 2, nb 8) | 25 | (b 16, lb 9, w 1, nb 5) | | 31 |
| **Total** | (101.4 overs) | **425** | (for 6 wkts dec) (71.2 overs) | | **311** |

## AUSTRALIA

| | | | | | |
|---|---|---|---|---|---|
| PJ Hughes | c Prior b Anderson | 4 | c Strauss b Flintoff | | 17 |
| SM Katich | c Broad b Onions | 48 | c Pietersen b Flintoff | | 6 |
| RT Ponting* | c Strauss b Anderson | 2 | b Broad | | 38 |
| MEK Hussey | b Flintoff | 51 | c Collingwood b Swann | | 27 |
| MJ Clarke | c Cook b Anderson | 1 | b Swann | | 136 |
| MJ North | b Anderson | 0 | b Swann | | 6 |
| BJ Haddin† | c Cook b Broad | 28 | c Collingwood b Flintoff | | 80 |
| MG Johnson | c Cook b Broad | 4 | b Swann | | 63 |
| NM Hauritz | c Collingwood b Onions | 24 | b Flintoff | | 1 |
| PM Siddle | c Strauss b Onions | 35 | b Flintoff | | 7 |
| BW Hilfenhaus | not out | 6 | not out | | 4 |
| Extras | (b 4, lb 6, nb 2) | 12 | (b 5, lb 8, nb 8) | | 21 |
| **Total** | (63 overs) | **215** | (107 overs) | | **406** |

| AUSTRALIA | O | M | R | W | | O | M | R | W |
|---|---|---|---|---|---|---|---|---|---|
| Hilfenhaus | 31 | 12 | 103 | 4 | | 19 | 5 | 59 | 0 |
| Johnson | 21.4 | 2 | 132 | 3 | | 17 | 2 | 68 | 0 |
| Siddle | 20 | 1 | 76 | 2 | | 15.2 | 4 | 64 | 2 |
| Hauritz | 8.3 | 1 | 26 | 0 | | 16 | 1 | 80 | 3 |
| North | 16.3 | 2 | 59 | 0 | | | | | |
| Clarke | 4 | 1 | 12 | 1 | (5) | 4 | 0 | 15 | 0 |

| ENGLAND | O | M | R | W | | O | M | R | W |
|---|---|---|---|---|---|---|---|---|---|
| Anderson | 21 | 5 | 55 | 4 | | 21 | 4 | 86 | 0 |
| Flintoff | 12 | 4 | 27 | 1 | | 27 | 4 | 92 | 5 |
| Broad | 18 | 1 | 78 | 2 | (4) | 16 | 3 | 49 | 1 |
| Onions | 11 | 1 | 41 | 3 | (3) | 9 | 0 | 50 | 0 |
| Swann | 1 | 0 | 4 | 0 | | 28 | 3 | 87 | 4 |
| Collingwood | | | | | | 6 | 1 | 29 | 0 |

Fall of wickets:

| | Eng | Aus | Eng | Aus |
|---|---|---|---|---|
| 1st | 196 | 4 | 61 | 17 |
| 2nd | 222 | 10 | 74 | 34 |
| 3rd | 267 | 103 | 147 | 78 |
| 4th | 302 | 111 | 174 | 120 |
| 5th | 317 | 111 | 260 | 128 |
| 6th | 333 | 139 | 311 | 313 |
| 7th | 364 | 148 | – | 356 |
| 8th | 370 | 152 | – | 363 |
| 9th | 378 | 196 | – | 388 |
| 10th | 425 | 215 | – | 406 |

Close of play:    Day 1: Eng (1) 364–6 (Strauss 161*, Broad 7*, 90 overs)
Day 2: Aus (1) 156–8 (Hauritz 3*, Siddle 3*, 49 overs)
Day 3: Eng (2) 311–6 (Flintoff 30*, Broad 0*, 71.2 overs)
Day 4: Aus (2) 313–5 (Clarke 125*, Haddin 80*, 86 overs)

Man of the Match: A Flintoff
**Result:**           **England won by 115 runs**

It was bizarre. But that was the point I'd reached. I knew I could get the job done, and I wanted to reach the limit as I did so.

In truth, my knee was a mess, just as my ankle had been. The first operation had been unsuccessful. Some bone fragments were still present and started to grow again and nobody could get them out. I had to have more and more operations, until eventually, after going under the knife in Holland, the situation became manageable. Dave Roberts was the one who researched the whole thing and effectively saved my career – not for the first time.

During matches, I survived on two sets of stimulants. First, the psychological need to find my limits. Secondly, industrial quantities of painkillers. It is a serious issue, how many pain-relieving drugs a sportsman should take. First, you have to stay within the rules. Secondly, you have to consider your own body. You are taking painkillers to mask pain that is happening for a reason. The pain is telling you there is a serious underlying issue. Ideally, you should fix the problem, not the symptom – though it doesn't always work out that way! Worst of all is the pain when they wear off – just terrible. You might get through the game, but you definitely pay later.

After the deep disappointment of 2006–07, I felt the

need to rectify things as much as I possibly could. Part of it was about proving something to the outside world. I also wanted to prove it to myself, even more strongly. That's why I played through the 2009 series, despite all the injuries. If I'd opted to have an operation after the first Test, I might have prolonged my career by two or three years. Those extra Tests possibly cost me three years at the top. But I thought it was the right thing to do at the time. Since then I've questioned it. But my conviction now is that it was the right thing to do.

Winning the Ashes in 2009 was totally different to 2005. In 2005 it was like riding a wave. No one expected us to win, so we could just have a go at them. It would always be fine. In 2009, every game could have been my last. Time was running out, chances were numbered.

There was also, from my perspective, a very different atmosphere socially. Partly, I had a bit of an agenda. While I was trying to prove stuff to myself, I don't think it detracted from what the team was trying to do. But when we won a game, I'd have a beer in my hand and I'd be looking around the dressing room for my mates. It was a very different group.

In the early days, playing for England was a double

thrill. You were playing for your country and you were doing it with your mates – Harmy, Keysey, Simon, Hoggy, Butch, Goughie. Inevitably, that changed. I really enjoyed some of the young players, people like Monty, Ravi Bopara, Tim Ambrose, and I tried to help them where I could. But there was a new team evolving. The conversations in the dressing room changed, the music changed.

It wasn't them, it was me. I was getting older. I realised I was never quite 'in'. They reacted to me differently. Which I didn't mind actually, being on the outside a bit. It was fine. But it wasn't as much fun. That's undeniable.


As a man, I'm quite young. As a sportsman, I'm very old. In some respects my body had worn out before I'd entirely grown up. That's professional sport for you.

Here's the irony. If I played now – if I could have a new knee, a new ankle, a new shoulder – I'd be a far better player.

As a batsman I'd be better, definitely. I would benefit from the fact that I can see it's only a game now. The times I struggled with batting were when I took it too seriously, like when Duncan got me to think too technically. Even last winter in Brisbane in the Big Bash, despite a lack of practice, after a few knocks I felt calm about my batting. I sleep well these days and cricket wouldn't change that.

I'm not sure I'd be as good a bowler. Why? Because in most parts of my life now the aggression has gone. Getting in people's faces, all that stuff, it's gone. There is still desire, but not aggression. I just roll with things, smile and get on with my life. There's no aggression there.

I do think I'd be a good captain if I did it again now. I don't think I'd necessarily be better tactically. But then I think the tactical element of cricket is wildly overstated anyway. It's just something people can spin out to fill the hours of commentary. In reality, most tactical changes happen within a narrow range. You might have three slips instead of four. You might have a third man. You might have a short leg or a man on the hook. But the most important part of a captain's impact is nothing to do with on-field tactics. And when it comes to man-management and getting the best out of players, I reckon I'd be much better at all that now.

I think I'm more tolerant and accepting of other people. Previously, I had my mates who I'd spend time with, and then there would be other players I couldn't stand. I'd be better at that now. That's where moving beyond sport has helped. Having worked in TV and different environments, I've worked with all sorts of men and women from every type of background, and it's broadened my outlook.

In sport, the dressing room can be very limited and narrow-minded. I used to think if someone didn't have the same interests as me then they were a little bit weird. In that world, if someone is different, there's a tendency to think something is wrong with them. But if you consider sport from the perspective of someone who is into dance or the arts, they might think it's weird that I like cricket. We like what we like, that's it.

Just as I've come to understand different tastes and interests, it is the same with different temperaments. I'm a lot more open-minded and accepting of people's different characters and their flaws than I was.

I've realised that I've got serious flaws myself and I've had to face them head-on. Face myself. As a result of that, I'd be more patient with a team. And I like to think I'd get more out of people by treating them differently, as individuals. Not trying to lead with bravado and bull, but by talking to people and understanding them a bit more. That's where the advantage lies for captains.

I don't have the same outlook as ten years ago. I'll give you an example. As a player, I must have made captains tear their hair out. Yet when I was captain, I sometimes lacked patience myself. I remember Saj Mahmood bowling an absolute shower during the 2006–07 Ashes. I said, 'What's going on?' He said, 'I can't find a good solid base.' That's the kind of bowling-biomechanics jargon I can't stand. So I said, 'Do you think there's any chance of you locating one today?' I whipped him off and that was it. You could say I lacked a degree of empathy.

I was at my best as a captain when I was spontaneous and wore the whole thing lightly. My most successful period as England captain was on the tour to India in early 2006. The best team talk, if you can call it that, was at Mumbai, in the third Test. Sachin Tendulkar was batting when we broke for lunch and the game was in the balance. I had a quick shower and as I was coming back into the dressing room, I switched the iPod player over to Johnny Cash's 'Ring of Fire'. Swinging my towel above my head, I started singing along at the top of my voice. One by one, the rest of the team joined in. On the way out to the middle, the great Tendulkar was so shocked by the mayhem that he put his head round the door and said, 'What the hell is going on in there?'

We were late out on to the pitch and when the umpire asked who was bowling, I said, 'Oh, haven't even thought about it. I'll have a bowl.' I got Tendulkar third ball. We bowled India out that afternoon, won the match and levelled the series – the first time since 1984–85 that an England team had come back from being behind in a Test series in India.

Another thing I've learnt is to avoid the dangers of becoming too goal-focused. My mind now is much stronger and clearer than when I was the Ashes captain. I've reached the point where I'm concerned with feeling good in that moment, not in the past, not in the future, just absorbed in what I'm doing right now. That mindset would have helped me as a captain. I was always trying to second-guess, to plan for every eventuality.

Sometimes, you just need to stay present in what is happening for this next ball, what is happening right now. Whether you're batting, bowling, at slip, or captain, I think you can look too far ahead. You look at winning the match, winning a series. What's the point? You can't affect the long term, only the next ball.

Above all, I've learnt a sense of perspective. Looking back, I feel for the missus. She used to get the worst of me. She didn't come out and celebrate when we won – that was with the lads – and I'd rock in at five in the morning, stinking and falling over. When we lost she'd see me there drowning my sorrows in the corner of the room. And then your career is all over. I bet she was happy when I retired.

Sometimes there'd be a problem with the house, or with something personal, and the view was always 'Oh, don't tell Fred, he's got a game tomorrow.'

And all these allowances are because you're doing this thing that's just a game! But it's blown out of all proportion – by you in your head, by the people watching, by the coaching staff. Everyone thinks it's far more important than it actually is. So everyone's got to fit in with your little world, your demands and needs. People talk about players needing to be selfish, but I don't buy into that. I think it's absolute nonsense. Then again, I don't think you realise until you've retired just how selfish you were. Not selfish about batting or anything like that. I mean actually selfish as a person.

It's quite embarrassing, really. There's something strange going on when your wife is told, 'You can come out on tour for this period of time and you can do this, but then we're doing this tonight, and then we are going to celebrate as a team, and here are the rules you've got to abide by.' It's weird. It was very much two different worlds. There was my world – cricket, the dressing room and the lads. And then there was family. And even when they travelled with me, it wasn't always easy to bridge the gap. Plus, I craved my own space as well.

You can understand why cricketers' marriages break down. If the shoe was on the other foot, I might have just turned around and said, 'You know what, sod this.'

I would add two final reflections about the captaincy experience and how it affected the last few years of my career. At first, I think I carried a lot of resentment, even about team-mates. I think that was one of the things that scuppered Kevin as well. When he lost the captaincy, he felt a sense of having been let down.

But then I thought, 'What's the point?' You've got to let it go. You get to a stage where you resent people and you're not quite sure why. You say to yourself, 'Why have I got a problem with him? Because he wrote some stuff in his book.' All that awkwardness over a few lines in a book? Is it really worth it? Of course it isn't.

I'm not going to get another bite of the cherry at captaining England, I know that. It's obviously not going to happen. But instead of channelling all the experiences and all the learning into captaincy, hopefully I'll be a better parent, which is far more important.

When I was young, I was single-minded and driven,

but I just want my children to be happy and I want to be able to support them in that. My three kids are certainly so different that I need three very different captaincy styles!

I'll definitely have some explaining to do when my kids get around to checking up on my younger days. I'm lining up my comments in advance. 'Perhaps it's better to start on page five of Google – after the drinking stories.' Also 'do as I say not as I did' could come in handy.

There is a glorious escapism about having children. You come home at night and they're not bothered if you batted badly or messed up professionally; they just want to see you. I'm big on discipline, I'm quite strict with them. But then I love switching to being a kid myself. Maybe the experts would say that's because my own childhood was influenced by playing a lot of serious cricket!

I have already written that the persona I built up as a cricketer covered up and reduced my emotions. Children, though, can cut through all that. When I watch them play sport or perform, I'm more nervous than I ever was as a player myself.

I lost my nan two years ago. We would sing 'Over the Rainbow' together when I was really young. I am quite good in a real crisis (and yet the silliest tiny thing can knock me off kilter) and when she died I slipped into the mode of doing all the practical things. I never really got a chance to mourn her. Then I saw my daughter performing 'Over the Rainbow' in a school play. At that point, thinking about how my daughter was singing the song I had sung with Nan for so many years, the emotions flooded out. It was beautiful.

Throughout my career, in cricket and beyond, I've been incredibly lucky with my marriage. I met Rachael in 2002 and that was the year my England career kicked on. Everything started to click. That was no coincidence. Professionally, I couldn't have done all the things I've done without her. She's always there for me.

She has helped me get over so many problems. When I was preoccupied with losing weight and started making myself throw up, I felt there was no one I could turn to. When I was able to speak to Rachael about it all, it made such a difference.

My first date with Rachael set the tone for our relationship, in rather an unusual way. I took her out on a Sunday evening. That day, the *News of the World* had run a story from the girl I had split up with. The headline was 'Flintoff's lovemaking like his bowling: hard, fast and straight.' The photo was terrible, too, with my head pictured in a crocodile's mouth.

How do you approach that kind of subject on a first date? Had she seen it or not? She had, as it turned out. But we just laughed about it. When something as potentially embarrassing as that happens on day one and you sail on past it, it's a pretty good sign that you're both able to see the funny side of life.

Thirteen years on, looking at my family today, I think, 'I could not have done any better.' That's one thing I have got right.

# 8

# THE GLASS HALF EMPTY

Winston Churchill had a great line about drink: 'I've taken more out of alcohol than alcohol has taken out of me.' I'd love to agree with that. But I'm not sure it's quite true for me.

Almost every sportsman has a story that paints drunkenness in a good light. We love to tell it, over and over. The names and places change, the script stays the same. Massive quantities of alcohol . . . a new freedom and flair . . . then, finally, triumph out on the pitch. You can see why everyone likes to repeat those tales at the bar and on the after-dinner-speaking circuit.

And, no surprise, I've got one of those stories too. In fact, it was after my first home Test hundred. More importantly, it was the start of me finding my voice as an England player. My breakthrough knock as a Test player came at Lord's in 2003, in the second Test against South Africa. I got on a roll after that and ended the summer as England's Man of the Series. That momentum stayed with me all the way to the famous Ashes summer of 2005.

Finding form came in an unconventional way, even by my standards. It was on the third day of the Test and we were losing, getting hammered by Graeme Smith again, who made 259 out of South Africa's 682. As a contest, the game was all over. We were going to get beaten; it was just a question of when. At the close of play, I was next man in.

Me and Steve Harmison didn't go back to our rooms; we went straight to the hotel bar. We ordered a couple of pints of Stella. We had one, then we had two, then we had three. It was Michael Vaughan's first game as captain and he passed us in the bar as he was going out for dinner. He could see the signs looked ominous.

'Just having a couple of pints, skip,' I called out, 'and then I'm going to bed because I'm next in tomorrow, aren't I?'

He said, 'All right, then.'

Vaughan came back at a reasonable hour and we're still there, me and Harmy, about ten pints in. Harmy's not bothered. But I'm meant to be an all-rounder, and Vaughany is seriously unamused. So I launch into this promise: 'I'm going to get a hundred tomorrow, I'll get a hundred tomorrow for you, skip. Tell you what, bet me, bet me that I don't get a hundred.'

Vaughany says, 'OK, how much do you want to bet?'

'I'll have a grand,' I said.

'No, come on, make it a proper bet, have two or three.'

There was a bit of back-and-forth before we eventually got a bit more sensible and shook on £100.

'Right then,' was the captain's last line, 'put your money where your mouth is.'

The next day, sitting on the balcony before I went in, I felt so rough. Jimmy Anderson, who could see I was in terrible shape, asked me how I was feeling.

'A bit dodgy, to be honest. But I'm going to have to pull something out the bag here. Vaughany is going to have a go at me if I don't do something special. I reckon I'm going to get my personal best here today. Definitely. I'll get a few here.'

In fact, I was sweating just sitting down.

When I got out to the middle, somehow I got through the first few balls. Then I thought to myself, 'I'm going to have a swing here, see what happens.' I hit a few, then I started playing shots I'd never played in my life before. I was running down the wicket to Shaun Pollock, whopping them over the leg-side.

Sweat was just pouring out of me. The kind of sweat

that tastes like pure alcohol when it drips into your mouth. Terrible. But it was one of those days when whatever I tried, it worked. Any shot I took on, I hit it.

Then I snapped my bat in half, and there's a famous photo of me holding a split bat, looking bemused. The expression came naturally at that stage and required no great acting skills, because I really didn't know what was going on. I just carried on swinging, hitting sixes and amusing myself. All this was against a top side: Ntini, Pollock, Hall. An extremely hung-over man smashing a hundred against the second-best team in the world.

I got 142. And my name was added to the honours board in the dressing room at Lord's. (Though, to be honest, I don't think anyone should get on that board whose performance happens in a game that his team loses.)

When I came off I had a little conversation with Michael Vaughan. I could tell we were fine, that he was OK.

'But you got away with it,' he added at the end.

'Yeah, and you owe me 100 quid,' I replied.

Vaughany gave a speech to the team after the game saying I'd saved him a few blushes by at least reducing the margin of the defeat. But he was absolutely right in what he'd said to me: I had got away with it.

Yet it's still a fact that the innings, for all its craziness,

# England v South Africa (2nd Test)

*Played at Lord's Cricket Ground, London, on 31 July–3 August 2003*

Umpires: SA Bucknor & DB Hair (TV: P Willey)
Referee: RS Madugalle
Toss: South Africa

## ENGLAND

| Batsman | 1st innings | | 2nd innings | |
|---|---|---|---|---|
| ME Trescothick | b Ntini | 6 | c Adams b Ntini | 23 |
| MP Vaughan* | c sub (ND McKenzie) b Ntini | 33 | c Pollock b Hall | 29 |
| MA Butcher | c Hall b Pollock | 19 | c Kirsten b Hall | 70 |
| N Hussain | b Hall | 14 | c Boucher b Ntini | 61 |
| A McGrath | c Kirsten b Hall | 4 | c Boucher b Pollock | 13 |
| AJ Stewart† | c Adams b Ntini | 7 | c Hall b Ntini | 0 |
| A Flintoff | c Adams b Ntini | 11 | st Boucher b Adams | 142 |
| AF Giles | c Pollock b Hall | 7 | c Pollock b Ntini | 23 |
| D Gough | c Adams b Pollock | 34 | c Adams b Pollock | 14 |
| SJ Harmison | b Ntini | 0 | c Hall b Ntini | 7 |
| JM Anderson | not out | 21 | not out | 4 |
| Extras | (b 5, lb 3, w 1, nb 3, p 5) | 17 | (b 6, lb 5, w 3, nb 17) | 31 |
| Total | (48.4 overs) | 173 | (107.1 overs) | 417 |

## SOUTH AFRICA

|  | | |
|---|---|---|
| GC Smith* | b Anderson | 259 |
| HH Gibbs | b Harmison | 49 |
| G Kirsten | b McGrath | 108 |
| HH Dippenaar | c Butcher b Giles | 92 |
| JA Rudolph | c Stewart b Flintoff | 26 |
| MV Boucher† | b Anderson | 68 |
| SM Pollock | not out | 10 |
| AJ Hall | not out | 6 |
| PR Adams | | |
| D Pretorius | | |
| M Ntini | | |
| Extras | (b 25, lb 21, w 5, nb 13) | 64 |
| Total | (for 6 wkts dec) (177 overs) | 682 |

| SOUTH AFRICA | O | M | R | W | | O | M | R | W |
|---|---|---|---|---|---|---|---|---|---|
| Pollock | 14.4 | 5 | 28 | 2 | | 29 | 7 | 105 | 2 |
| Ntini | 17 | 3 | 75 | 5 | | 31 | 5 | 145 | 5 |
| Pretorius | 4 | 0 | 20 | 0 | (5) | 3 | 0 | 16 | 0 |
| Hall | 10 | 4 | 18 | 3 | (3) | 24 | 6 | 66 | 2 |
| Adams | 3 | 0 | 19 | 0 | (4) | 20.1 | 1 | 74 | 1 |

| ENGLAND | O | M | R | W |
|---|---|---|---|---|
| Gough | 28 | 3 | 127 | 0 |
| Anderson | 27 | 6 | 90 | 2 |
| Harmison | 22 | 3 | 103 | 1 |
| Flintoff | 40 | 10 | 115 | 1 |
| Giles | 43 | 5 | 142 | 1 |
| Butcher | 6 | 1 | 19 | 0 |
| McGrath | 11 | 0 | 40 | 1 |

Fall of wickets:

| | Eng | SA | Eng |
|---|---|---|---|
| 1st | 11 | 133 | 52 |
| 2nd | 35 | 390 | 60 |
| 3rd | 73 | 513 | 186 |
| 4th | 77 | 580 | 208 |
| 5th | 85 | 630 | 208 |
| 6th | 96 | 672 | 208 |
| 7th | 109 | – | 297 |
| 8th | 112 | – | 344 |
| 9th | 118 | – | 371 |
| 10th | 173 | – | 417 |

Close of play:  Day 1: SA (1) 151–1 (Smith 80*, Kirsten 9*, 41 overs)
Day 2: SA (1) 412–2 (Smith 214*, Dippenaar 11*, 110 overs)
Day 3: Eng (2) 129–2 (Butcher 33*, Hussain 36*, 36 overs)

Man of the Match: GC Smith & M Ntini
**Result:**     **South Africa won by an innings and 92 runs**

marked the beginning of a totally new phase in my England career. After that alcohol-fuelled day at Lord's, my batting was different. It was really different. My attitude towards how I was going to bat changed completely. Another big factor was the hundreds of hours of hard work I'd put in that summer with Mike Watkinson at Lancashire.

Just standing there, worrying about where my off-stump was, trying to leave a few, hanging in and trying to survive – I'd finished with all that. I was going to go in there to hit the ball. That's what I could do, what I did best, and that's how I was going to play. So, yes, it would be true to say that drinking unlocked something fundamental in my performance. It was one big night out that kick-started the really productive period of my Test career.

I'll tell you another story, a much less happy one, about me and drinking. It was during my captaincy in 2006–07, when we were losing and playing awfully.

In one sense, you could make a case that my captaincy might not have made much difference on the Ashes tour. We had injuries, players were out of form, Duncan Fletcher was at the end of his tenure (and his tether). Above all, Australia were just miles better than us in every way. I think even Andrew Strauss, who ended up being the right man to lead England, has said that he dodged a bullet by not being made captain in 2006–07 when I got the job.

But that would only be half the story of that tour. When I'd been just a player, I'd always been able to switch off. As a captain, I couldn't. I carried my worries and problems with me everywhere. It's also true that I was drinking too much. And not just heavy drinking, but the wrong kind of heavy drinking. That story of me drinking before batting at Lord's is one thing: with a great friend, in high spirits, taking away pressure, smiling at the world. That can work for you sometimes and it did on that occasion. My drinking in Australia was the other kind. I'd retreat to my room and hit the minibar. It was escapism again, but of course you don't actually escape anything. The next day all the same problems are still there, only amplified. And you've got a headache.

Looking back on it all today, with the perspective I couldn't find at the time, I'm almost embarrassed that I let the whole situation go so far. The Ashes is only a handful of burnt bails. Some people in the world do things that really matter. Others have proper struggles. I lost sight of all that.

In the World Cup that followed – Fredalo and all – it was obvious that there was a lot wrong with me. When

I got wickets, I'd just stand there, I couldn't even celebrate. I felt nothing. I had no emotions either way, positive or negative. I felt like a zombie. When team-mates
jumped on my back celebrating, I wanted to shout, 'Get
off me!' I'd just stand there, not part of it, then walk back
to my mark.

The point I'm making is that if you pick your evidence
carefully, it's easy to make a case one way or the other
with drink. The truth is much more complex. Yes, drink
was bound up with my career, both the ups and the
downs. But now I'm happier to live without it.

The first thing about my strange relationship with drink
is that I genuinely like it. I like a pint. I love red wine.
In cricket, I'd drink to celebrate and that's good. But I
also drank after my losses as well. Just any excuse. When
you can say that, you have a problem.

The culture of cricket when I started was a drinking
culture. It was only a few years after the days when a
tray of beer would be brought in at lunch. They'd have
a bitter and then bowl an eight-over spell. In my early
days, the twelfth man would bring up a tray of drinks at
the end of a day's play. Forget energy drinks or rehydra-
tion, as is the fashion now. The only question was 'Lager

or bitter?' You'd have a couple of pints in the dressing room and then move on from there. When I started drinking, I found I was 'good at it'. It led to a new kind of acceptance in the dressing room. That was the way it was in that era.

There were times when I didn't drink nearly as much as people thought. But I didn't mind them thinking that. I wanted people to think I was different. I played a lot on personality, and the drinking and the occasional cigarettes were all part of the act, part of my stage persona. If I turned up in the morning having had a few drinks the night before, there was almost a mystique about it – 'How does he do that?' – from both my team-mates and the opposition. Drink was one of the ways I'd do things different in the dressing room. When everyone was having a protein shake, I'd have a pint, just to make a point.

After 2005, for a period of time drink became intertwined with expectations. It was also a way of coping with some of the unusual social situations I found myself in. At a World Cup party once, David Beckham introduced me to Puff Daddy. I was pretty far gone, to be honest, and I didn't know what to call him, so I said, 'All right, Puff.' And he said, 'My name's Sean.' And I said, 'All right, Sean Puff.'

It was a strange phase. I was caught up in a whirl of social events. It was not something I'd gone looking for. I'd never thought being in that crowd was the be-all and end-all. However, given that all I knew was the cricketing world, it was something different and I was intrigued by it. So I started going to parties and functions. I got bored of it very quickly. A lot of the people were just superficial. That was evident. And I didn't really feel comfortable in that environment. So I'd drink just to get through it. That was how 'celebrity culture', for want of a better phrase, reinforced my tendency to drink.

In other areas of my life, the people I knocked around with also had a taste for drink. The mates I see in Preston, they live for the weekend. They work hard all week and they go at it at the weekend. That's where the fun happens. There's always someone getting a bit of stick, copping it. And drink plays a part. In a way, they are creating a dressing-room environment in their lives, too.

There was also, ridiculous as it now sounds, a competitive dimension to my drinking, certainly when I was younger. Who could take the most, who could hold his grog, all that macho stuff. Everybody would laugh at the person who was behind, the first to throw up. When I deconstruct it now as an adult, it's hard to get your head around it. Why were we laughing at the guy who can't speak or who falls over or who's wet his pants because he's so drunk? Where's the humour, why are we ridiculing him? It's weird when you think about it, but that's how it was.

I know drinking doesn't help with injuries. But it was also true, in my case, that injuries led me to drink. It took so much out of me, trying to get fit all the time. I would finally get back into shape, only to break down again and it was back to square one. I would drink to get through that disappointment and annoyance.

Then your reputation starts to follow you around. I'd be having dinner in a restaurant and three pints would suddenly appear on a tray. Another diner in the restaurant would have sent them to my table with a message – 'Enjoy these!' – and I'd look up to see someone in the corner waving enthusiastically.

Total strangers always wanted to talk about drinking. People felt the need to come up to me and tell me about a big night, 'Oh, you'd have loved last night, I went out and drank this and that . . .' They enjoyed telling me about some embarrassing thing they'd done when they were drunk. And people assumed – wrongly – that every time I was out I was automatically up for a big night. Someone's always on a big night, of course, and they'd just take it for granted that I wanted to go on it with them, to join in the fun.

When it comes to alcohol, I never really grew up. In other areas in my life, I think I have. But when it comes to alcohol, I'm still like a giddy toddler who's had his first bite of chocolate or thinks he's seeing Father Christmas tomorrow. Something in me lights up. And it's not for the better.

Thinking about it now, it's hard to explain some of the things I'd get up to; it really is baffling. We used to have Sambuca. Why? It's horrible. And then we'd set it on fire. Put it in your mouth, set fire to it, end up with massive burns on your lips.

We'd make up drinks – the worse, the better. There was one drink we came up with in a London pub. We called it the Grenade. You take a pint glass and put Red Bull in the bottom, then get two shot glasses and pop them in the pint glass, one with Jägermeister and one with a whisky, all wedged in. Then you pull out the whisky and neck it and the other shot glass drops down, and you drink the resulting Jägerbomb. It got ridiculous. I was thirty-four, thirty-five years old at this stage, a grown man.

There was always another level you could go to. So we'd get rid of the Red Bull and just use any old messy series of shots. And this is fun? I never even liked shots. Bought loads of them. Never liked any of them. I can't really explain that.

More importantly, I realised a while ago that drinking was the motivation for too many things in my life. I started asking why I did stuff. Why do I go and watch football? Oh yeah, I get a pint. Why do I play golf? Because I get a pint at the end. But why am I bothering walking round eighteen holes first? Why don't I just go and have a pint? Everything had become entangled with booze. It all came back to having a pint.

Well, it's not really what I want to do. Not now. I think I've just had enough of that particular mask I used to wear. I genuinely have. I became a liability during TV interviews if I'd had a big night. Maybe it was funny for a while, but then the joke started to wear a bit thin.

I don't touch drink now, for lots of reasons. First, it can turn me into an idiot. Secondly, I get really fat when I drink and I don't want to get really fat. Above all, I don't drink now because I've used drink in the past to change my feelings. Whether it was feelings of insecurity or depression, I'd drink in the hope that I wouldn't go on feeling that way.

Three or four pints in, you feel like cock of the walk. But then you keep going and you end up in oblivion. And the next day you wake up and, however bad your problems felt without a hangover, with a hangover they're always a lot worse.

It's one thing drinking to celebrate. Another if you're drinking to hide. You're trying to escape, to run from something. So there is always a better answer. Another reason I don't touch it now is because if I do, I'm not the type who can have just one or two pints. I'd sooner have a glass of Coke. If I am going to drink, one's never enough. So I genuinely think I'm better off without it.

Even now, with parents on the school run – parents I don't know that well – when I see them after they've had a massive night out, they feel they have to tell me everything that happened, everything they got up to. The story always starts with, 'Oh, you'd have loved it . . .' And I'll say, 'I probably wouldn't have, really. I'm a bit old for all that.'

That flummoxes them.

\* \* \*

It's how a lot of people see me, I know. On social media I might say I've been at the gym and I'll get abuse from people saying, 'You soft ----. You should have been out drinking!' It's obviously the reputation I've created and, fair enough, at times I've played up to it. But it's not me now.

There seems to be a time lag with reputations, sadly. It takes a while for people to catch up with reality. I recently bumped into my old mate Neil Fairbrother, who used to be my manager. He was visiting Stuart Broad at a London hotel after Broady had just pulled out of an England sponsor's event, feeling a bit worse for wear. So I tweeted Stuart mischievously, saying I hope he enjoyed his bed bath and that he felt better soon. The next day the newspapers reported that I had been out drinking with Broady until 7 a.m. Total nonsense, and they set the record straight the following week, but by then it had been reported in most other newspapers. I know I've done silly things, but that isn't an excuse for people just to make things up about me.

Socially, being around drinking is not something I dodge. I can be around it, I can drink Coke without worrying about that. I just wish they'd invent a few more exciting non-alcoholic drinks, something that can see you through the evening. Because even I can't drink five pints of Coke! As for the other options, they're even worse. You look a bit of a twit drinking a cocktail at the best of times. You look a massive twit drinking a mock-tail with an umbrella on top.

How would my career have panned out without drink? It got me into a lot of trouble, no question. When things went wrong for me, especially professionally, I was usually drinking. But I enjoyed it a lot, too. And at times, drink certainly helped give me a release, rightly or wrongly. I'm not suggesting that's what people should do. But for me, it really did.

I think that's quite typical, actually. Drink is entangled with lots of careers among driven people. 'A man who drinks,' Tennessee Williams said, 'is two people, one grabbing the bottle, the other fighting him off it.' But did you really need it? Or did you persuade yourself you needed it? And how honest are you about that?

Would I have been a better or worse player if I hadn't ever touched alcohol? I often ask myself the question. I certainly would have been different, very different. I reckon I'd have been like everyone else is today.

But better or worse? I really couldn't say. Maybe Andrew would have taken over, and Fred been relegated. And I'm not at all sure that Andrew would have been a natural professional sportsman – he'd have been too self-conscious, anxious and unassuming.

Sometimes your strengths and weaknesses can't be separated so easily. What I can say is that I wouldn't swap my career with anyone else's. I've enjoyed my lot.

When you think about it, I've now ended up losing my two hobbies: playing cricket and drinking. I've had to learn other ways to spend my free time.

# 9

# THE PERFORMER

I T might look as though my career after cricket – one minute a professional boxer, the next presenting on TV and doing theatre gigs – has taken one surprising turn after another. And it's true that I am always tackling new things. But there is also a common thread: the need to perform, to find new challenges, to push myself and find my limits. I've always had a desire – perhaps 'need' is a better term than 'desire' – to throw myself in at the deep end.

There is that line: 'It is not the critic who counts; not the man who points out how the strong man stumbles, or where the doer of deeds could have done them better. The credit belongs to the man who is actually in the arena.' That's dead right.

I was much the same as a young kid. Maybe it comes from my time at school, when I'd just try to get through the day with my teeth intact. From the schoolyard onwards, I've always put myself in situations I'm not sure I can get through.

I don't like people telling me I can't do things. That's when I'm at my most dangerous, when people write me off. I like the fear it gives me. I like being on the edge, or as close to it as I can get. Just knowing that I'm taking something on. I'd always sooner be the person in the middle of something who is an open target to the critics. I've always hated people on the sidelines who take potshots at the ones who have a go.

The first TV show I made was a series for ITV, just after I retired from Tests in 2009. It was called *Flintoff Versus the World*. The idea was that I would attempt a series of extreme sports – rodeo riding, jumping out of aeroplanes, paragliding, cliff diving. I thought, 'Yeah, it looks fun. It's six weeks having a laugh.'

We started out in Acapulco, then made our way across America and Canada. The plan was to put me into the most terrifying situations the production team could dream up. The good thing was that I wouldn't be doing it alone. For each episode there would be someone else to share the suffering. So for the first episode in Mexico – *lucha libre* wrestling and a dive off the cliffs in Acapulco – I thought who better than my old cricketing pal Darren Gough. I also made some good friends in the crew – Paul 'Mungo' Mungeam, the cameraman, is one of my best mates. I needed them, to be honest, as the central theme of the programme, in each day's filming, was to come as close to killing someone as possible!

The oddest part of the experience was how quickly I became acclimatised to this as a normal professional state of affairs. At breakfast, planning the day ahead, the conversation would go like this: 'Oh, what are we doing this week?' And they'd reply, 'Well, you're doing some freestyle wrestling in the dodgy backstreets of Mexico City, then we'll shovel you out of a plane, and after that we're chucking you on a bucking rodeo bull.'

And after a while, I'd just think, 'Oh, sure, OK.'

The wrestling involved one classic moment. Me and Goughy wrestled together against a Mexican tag-team duo. But I aggravated an old rib injury, so I couldn't take part in the wrestling bout later in the evening.

We were in a rough corner of Mexico City, with hired thugs protecting us – gangsters, essentially – to make sure we were going to be safe, or as safe as possible. At the gym about a thousand people had gathered to watch the fight. When me and Goughy were unveiled to the crowd, we got the biggest boos I'd ever heard.

Goughy had picked the outfit in order to make me look like Freddie Mercury. Kind of him. I was wearing a red Lycra T-shirt and white Lycra leggings. But somehow we had to telegraph that I was injured and couldn't wrestle, so I'd wrapped a white bandage around my ribs – hoping the crowd didn't kick off about me pulling out.

Because this was wrestling, which is supposed to be scripted and preplanned, we'd plotted a routine. Goughy had been practising it. He would go into the fight, get thrown over, do a couple of runs, jump over the other fella, go under him once, then the other guy would pick him up, turn him over and smash him on to the deck. And then that would be it, show over.

Sadly, it didn't quite work out like that. I don't know if it was the crowd atmosphere, but in the ring the other wrestler's juices started flowing and he really battered Goughy. He was slapping him across the face and then he was climbing on the top rope and jumping on him.

I was at the side of the ring wetting myself, banging on the canvas in fits of laughter. Then the trouble started. This woman decided to abuse me – in Spanish, obviously. So I started giving it back.

At this point, in retrospect, I can see the absurdity of having an argument in which neither party speaks the other's language. When I told her to 'Shut up, you old cow,' which I suppose was a bit strong, her husband gestured that he was going to shoot me. Bang.

At this point I realised that nothing about the current situation was terribly encouraging. Goughy had been in the ring for about twenty minutes getting smashed up. The fight was beginning to spill outside the ring into the crowd. And a Mexican thug was gesturing to shoot me.

Time to leave the ring, pronto.

As our opponents celebrated, Goughy couldn't resist one last act of showmanship, grabbing the microphone and giving a rousing speech straight out of *Rocky* – 'Me and my friend here, it's been amazing. Thank you, Mexico!' – the only problem being that none of them understood a word of English and they began a distinctly unamused slow handclap. We disappeared double quick to the dressing room.

All in all, I think that experience is best described as hit and miss. The next day we got up and went diving off Acapulco's famous cliffs, which was fabulous.


Another episode involved me having a drag race on the strip in Las Vegas, live on ESPN, with about 25,000 in the crowd watching me take on the Irish boxer Steve Collins. It was great fun in the end. But to start with they had to change my car: I wouldn't fit in a conventional drag car. I had to get a more traditional big car with a huge engine sticking out of the front. That was amazing.

My brother came out to watch the Las Vegas stuff and had a great time. I love my brother, but even he would admit that he's a bit tight about money. So he was really chuffed that he could have free drinks all night at the casinos. He reckons he just pretended to play the slots, downed the free drinks and spent maybe $25 all in. He was very happy with himself.

As for working with the basketball player Dennis Rodman, that was . . . interesting.

The challenge in his episode was to become a fighter pilot over Laguna Beach in California. Perhaps he's skint, Dennis. All I know is that when he was approached for a week's work filming the programme, his agent asked for £70,000. They offered £6,000. He said, 'We'll do it for £7,000.'

I first met him the day before we started filming, hanging out with his mates. Not a promising start. Rodman was in a terrible state, in a bar lighting up bank notes. Fifty-dollar bills, just lighting them up, one by one. He was acting the big cheese, throwing a wad of money around.

Next thing, Rodman says it's all off, he's not doing the programme. I eventually managed to talk him around and we arranged to meet at nine o'clock the next morning to get started. The following day we were waiting as agreed in the hotel car park. No sign of Rodman.

David 'Rooster' Roberts, my old physio from Lancashire, had joined the crew for the trip. Rooster hates lateness, thinks it's just rude. So Rooster is kicking off: 'Where is he, this ------- Rodman? Where is he, this -----? I'm going to go and get him from his room.' The director is desperately trying to talk him down to prevent a scene.

Ten o'clock passes, eleven o'clock, and we're still all waiting in the car park. Rodman finally surfaces at one o'clock, battered, as though he's taken everything. I knew he had a colourful history of drugs, drink and other abuses. What I didn't expect was that his excessive lifestyle would be so apparent at the first shoot.

So I've got a bit of a hangover and Dennis is off his box. What do you do in those circumstances? Go up and fly aeroplanes, of course.

First, there's a training session, so that air-force veterans can talk us through how to fly. But Rodman is so far gone he just keeps saying 'You old fucker, you old fucker' to the instructor. Finally, we're taken up in these planes and then given the controls to have a dogfight. If you get your plane to 'lock on' you score a point. (Think *Top Gun*, basically.) That's the idea, anyway. But I'm throwing up in a bag because I feel terrible and Rodman's plane is just all over the place. I can chalk that one up as an experience unlikely to be repeated: a dogfight with a six-foot-ten cross-dressing ex-husband of Carmen Electra and ex-boyfriend of Madonna.

It was a bad start to a week that deteriorated steadily from there. You'd be walking down the street with him and some driver would stop his car just to hurl abuse at him. Others would shout out that he was a legend. In the end, the best activity we could think of with Dennis was going ten-pin bowling. The real pleasure was seeing him off and saying goodbye.

There was one unfortunate side effect of making that series – the drinking. Every day was seriously adrenaline-fuelled, so almost every night was a big night – partly from high sprits, partly to come down from the high of the challenge. The programmes, however, weren't shown in the order they were filmed. So the viewer must have felt very confused. One minute I look quite fit, then I've suddenly gained two stone, then the next week I'm back down to a reasonable weight. It looked so ridiculous that people must have thought I'd been yo-yo dieting.

The last night of filming was the biggest of all, a real monster. Somehow an American couple attached themselves to our group and I wasn't sure what they wanted. Eventually, at about 3 a.m., this American fella said to me, 'What are you doing later?' I said, 'Oh, we've got an early flight.' He said, 'Well, would you like to come back with my wife and me?' I said, 'Not sure what you mean.' He elaborated: 'Would you like to sleep with my wife?' 'No, I wouldn't actually,' I replied. 'Not really on my agenda, that. We don't do that in Preston.' Then I couldn't resist adding, 'But just as a matter of interest, if I was to say yes, what would you do?' 'I'd just watch,' he answered.

Quite an odd chap, I thought, so I told him to get lost. What kind of world had I got myself into?

Around this time I left my old management company. I found that very difficult. I'd been with ISM for a long time and Neil Fairbrother, my Lancashire team-mate turned agent, was one of my best friends. He was fine about it all, though I found the decision hard. It wasn't easy to part company with a lifelong friend, someone I had admired as a team-mate and who had always backed me as a player. But I was learning what every ex-professional athlete has to confront one day: I needed a plan for the rest of my life. Even if nothing would be quite the same as cricket, I had to forge a new direction, find new challenges. Richard Thompson and Katie Lydon at M&C Saatchi Merlin have been great at that.

I blame myself for giving up too much control to my initial agents. It is a criticism of me, not them. It is a danger for many young sportsmen. You need to grow up and take control of your life. I wouldn't quite say I couldn't buy an airline ticket when I retired. But I wasn't used to normal, everyday life. I ceded too much control to other people. I should have done the mundane things myself, the stuff of ordinary life.

Some other people I do hold accountable. One 'investment adviser', who made the worst decisions of the lot, ingratiated himself as a family friend. Then he just disappeared. He made his money, lost mine, and then I never saw him again. He didn't even have the decency to come and see me to explain the mess he'd created.

\* \* \*

After *Flintoff Versus the World* I made a programme called *Alone in the Wild*. I had to spend a week on my own in a tent in the Okavango Delta in Botswana.

I had two days' training – about how to catch food and what to eat – but I didn't really listen to the instructions. I'm not always brilliant at listening. The theory sounded good: the landscape so wild – it wasn't designated parkland, it was just scrubland – that if you came in contact with any animals, they wouldn't even know what you were. As they'd never seen humans, they wouldn't like the smell of you and they'd leave you alone. That was what you were relying on for your safety. But you still had to keep moving every two nights because the hyenas would edge closer.

It was great. I pitched my tent by the river. As I didn't have food or a water supply, I drank out of the river. I went walking, got lost, filmed elephants. No camera crew, just me doing the filming. I had a tracker, to keep an eye on me, a Botswana lad, but I never saw him. Even he wouldn't hang around at night, though; he said it was far too dangerous.

The most hair-raising moment was filming the elephants. I was stood on a termite mound, filming these elephants in the distance. I like elephants. Even though they're really big – and I know this may sound ridiculous – they can hide very well. I was filming the group when all of a sudden this other elephant appeared from behind a tree, or so it seemed. A stand-off with an elephant about twenty yards away. For Christ's sake! But I was also thinking, 'I'm getting some amazing footage here – he's flapping his ears very enthusiastically.'

When I got back, I spoke to the tracker about it all.

'You did well with that elephant, because he was just about to charge you,' he told me. 'Yeah, he was ready. He'd raised the final warning shot when you started backing off.'

'Was he?' I said. I had no idea.

Another day, I climbed a tree. And afterwards the tracker again said, 'Oh, you did really well, really well.'

'What do you mean?' I said.

'Well, you know when you climbed that tree to avoid the lion? That was a really good effort, that.'

'What are you on about?' I said. 'I didn't see a lion. I just climbed a tree to have a look around.'

'Well, the lion went past you and then I had a stand-off.'

Oh right. Glad I hadn't realised.


I did another series for Discovery called *Freddie Flintoff Goes Wild*. I went to four different types of wild terrain and watched the people and wildlife that live there. In Tanzania I joined the Maasai tribe on the hunt for the great wildebeest migration. I collected bushtucker with Aboriginals in the Northern Territories of Australia. Then I tracked orangutans and pygmy elephants with the Dusun natives in Borneo. Finally I went to the heart of the Discovery Islands in Canada, where I searched out wolves, bears, deer and cougars.

As a life experience it was extraordinary, but I wish I was doing them all now, not four years ago. I'm more confident at making TV, so they'd be better programmes. Still, I loved doing it. In some ways, it would have been even better if I could have had those experiences entirely on my own, without any cameras at all. But you can't have one without the other: that's the nature of opportunities that come from TV.

It scares me in a way, because I don't know how far I might go. I don't really get worried about things that ought to worry me. We did a parachute jump for one show and on the way up everyone else was terrified. I fell asleep in the plane, not nervous at all. But then at other times something really tiny will eat away at me, like a lost rucksack worth six quid.

I've also enjoyed taking part in several series of *A League of Their Own*, with James Corden, Jamie Redknapp and

Jack Whitehall. (Georgie Thompson and John Bishop were in the first four series.) I turned it down initially – I was still hoping to play cricket at the time – and then decided to do it a week before filming began. It's fun. And I think that having fun is the key to the success of the show.

The programme I'm proudest of is *The Hidden Side of Sport*, a documentary for the BBC about depression. We had a budget for fifteen days; it ended up taking thirty. For the second half of the schedule we were all – the crew as well as me – working effectively for free. Everyone bought into it as a passion project. We wanted to get it right. And it was worth it.

I'm not a do-gooder. And I'm not preaching. But judging from the overall reaction to that programme, it was something that helped people. That is always going to be more fulfilling than jumping out of a plane.

There was no set agenda or fixed narrative for the programme in my mind. I wanted to listen to other public figures who'd had mental-health issues. When I reflected on their stories, my own problems took on a clearer focus.

One of the interviewees was the boxer Ricky Hatton. I admired Ricky and I'd been a fan of his. Our careers were at their heights at the same time, both of us based around Manchester. As I was playing in the 2005 Ashes, Ricky was beating Kostya Tszyu on his way to becoming *Ring* magazine's fighter of the year. We often bumped into each other and got on well. He was a wonderfully brave, proud fighter whose defeats, especially against Floyd Mayweather Jr, took their toll on his sense of perspective and self-confidence. He ended up having three further professional fights, despite suffering from depression.

Ricky described how his depression was magnified by drinking. Evenings that began with him feeling as if his old confidence was flooding back would end with him sat in the corner of the pub sobbing in front of his friends, having to be put into a taxi. 'It's very hard for a man,' he said, 'especially a professional boxer, to go to someone and say, "I've got a problem, I need help."'

That interview underlined the difference between perception and reality when it comes to mental health. If it can affect Ricky Hatton – Jack the Lad and hard as nails – it can hit anyone. And, in the same way, if he can talk honestly about it, so, hopefully, can other people. To have that conversation with Ricky was brilliant. He opened up and so did I.

I told Ricky about something that happened during my

time as England captain in Australia in 2006–07. We were 3–0 down by Christmas, the Ashes already gone. On Christmas Eve, which is supposed to be a happy time, I had a few drinks with my dad. As Dad was about to leave, I broke down crying. I started saying, 'I'm sorry, I've let you down. I've tried my best. I can't give any more, can't try any harder than I am.' I was in floods of tears and then my dad started crying too.

After that series, I don't think I ever got back to the player I had once been. That 2006–07 period knocked me so much that it was always going to be impossible to put it completely behind me. I dusted myself down and I came back. But only to a degree. I was never quite the same player.

I hadn't expected to reveal so much about myself in *The Hidden Side of Sport*. My great friend Steve Harmison suffered for ten years with depression. All those years, spending time with him – it was almost a kind of therapy for me. I'd talk to him about what he was going through, yet neither of us even realised that I was going through a very similar kind of thing.

Making the programme, as I was listening to others talking about depression, I kept thinking, 'You know what? I've had that since I was a kid.' I could identify with so much of what they said. I'd just lacked the knowledge and the language to understand what I'd felt. When I spoke to these people and revealed things about myself, it was a relief to open up.

One strange thing about depression is that it doesn't always strike when you expect. You can be going through the worst time ever, professionally or personally, and you're fine. Then you might be having a good spell and all of a sudden something will send you completely out of kilter.

We interviewed the snooker player Graeme Dott for the programme. He won the 2006 World Championships and then had the worst year of his life. He clearly had a susceptibility to depression, and that was triggered by the death of his manager and his wife suffering a major health issue. He broke down in one match completely.

The interview up in Scotland was both challenging and upsetting. Initially it started out very light-hearted. For some reason the crew and I were in a silly mood, the kind that follows from being over-tired. Graeme showed us his snooker table in his converted garage. Then we had to empty almost every lamp out of his house and rearrange it all in the snooker room to get the lighting right. And Graeme was in the thick of it, helping out, messing around.

Somehow we then had to do a sharp turn and go from all that to talking about depression. Which Graeme did brilliantly. He was so honest about what it had done to him. But after dragging him into that territory, we suddenly had to pack up and leave. I think he'd really enjoyed us coming round and talking to him. As we drove away, he stood outside the house waving us off, like a child waving his parents off on the train.

It was so sad. In retrospect, I think we misjudged it. We really should have asked him to come out for dinner with us afterwards.

The programme took us into unexpected territory. We'd gone to LA for various interviews and Piers Morgan had given me Vinnie Jones's number as a potential interviewee. I'd never met Vinnie, didn't know him at all, though I knew that he'd had some mental-health problems. So I texted him to make contact. But what do you say then? 'I'm making a programme about depression and I thought you'd be good on it?' It's an awkward conversation. It's such a private subject. But after we had exchanged text messages I rang him.

It was like a whirlwind coming down the phone at me. I'd scarcely finished explaining the idea behind the documentary when he launched into a plan: 'All right, Freddie, I've got a poker night at seven tonight, come at half six, we can have half an hour or forty-five minutes, then you can join the poker.'

We drove to Vinnie's house on Mulholland Drive in LA. It was so bizarre. We set up in his kitchen and I'd prepared all the things I wanted to ask in my head. I don't like writing things down. I prefer to keep the essence of it in my head and then just see where it goes. So we started talking about the 'Crazy Gang' when he was a footballer at Wimbledon, and how dressing-room culture has changed so much; how when we started out young players would get picked on for any weakness or flaw. He also credited his dog with saving his life when he was in a particularly depressed spell.

Between these revelations, we had to keep stopping filming because Vinnie's guests were arriving for the poker night, walking through the kitchen and out on to the patio to his cabana-style party room. I'd ask a question and then Michael Greco from *EastEnders* would walk through. Then another question and it would be a top football manager. Then, hang on a minute, it's Quentin Tarantino. Turns out, Tarantino lived next door. Finally, three porn stars arrived, including Keiran Lee from Derby, the lad who insured his penis with Lloyd's of London for a million dollars.

And I'm thinking, 'Hang on a minute! I'm trying to make a documentary on depression and we're just getting to the point where Vinnie is about to spill his heart out and then this procession begins!' It was one of the strangest days of my life.

The trip included a visit to watch LA Galaxy, in a box as guests of David Beckham. It wasn't a proper league match and, to be honest, I don't think it was David's finest game. He'd been surfing all morning and thought it was a day off. He was tired but his team-mates kept trying to get the ball to him. So he basically stood in the middle of the park, laying off passes. You could have rubbed his footmarks out of the grass afterwards.

He's a super guy and we had a really nice evening out for dinner. Then at about ten o'clock he said, 'Do you want to come down the house?' It turned out he was renting Steven Spielberg's place in Malibu. In one way, it was a completely normal scene – he made us some food in the kitchen while his missus was feeding the baby. But the next minute we were sipping beer and watching football in the cinema room – Steven Spielberg's cinema room! Behind us was an old projector and a series of film reels. It was quite surreal.

It's a revealing episode, the story of making *The Hidden Side of Sport*. It was surprising, unintended, emotional, memorable and, for me, above all a psychological turning point – all rolled into one.

Along the way I've also made radio programmes for the BBC, including an extended interview for BBC 5 Live with Kevin Pietersen before the 2013 Ashes. In our interview, Kevin made an interesting comment that resonated with me. 'I've got this reputation for being confident,' he explained, 'yet I go and do all these psychology tests and I find that I'm an introvert.'

How would I answer if I was interviewing myself and I asked the same question? My first reaction is to say that I'm an extroverted introvert. Is that possible? My natural instinct is to be an introvert, there is no doubt about that. But there is a performer in my character, too, and that's where the extroversion expresses itself. It is usually a performance.

What I've gradually learnt is to recognise the distinction between when I'm just holding a conversation and when I've tripped over into performing.

Often when I'm the subject of an interview or I'm making an appearance, I'll perform. They're expecting a certain persona and I'll go along with that. So you do perform, and you feel yourself doing it. But sometimes that switch gets flicked when I'm just around my mates or in the dressing room, and then all of a sudden it's tits and teeth everywhere. It's really odd. It's acting. I acted when I was a bowler, I had a persona. This is just a different sort of acting.

There have also been times, though, when I've made programmes using my other voice, when it felt like a normal conversation, not 'presenting' but just chatting and seeing what comes out of it. That's how it was in the documentary on depression. With a lot of stuff I've done, I was always thinking of a one-liner to entertain people. Not with that programme. That's one reason I'm proud of it. It came from the other side of my personality.

# 10

# LICENCE TO BOX

How did I end up in a professional boxing ring, fighting an ex-con from the American Deep South who'd been shot four times? Even by my standards, my brief spell as a pro boxer was weird. I can see now that it is also revealing. In fact, the story of my short time boxing is a pretty decent summary of my career in cricket. It's as if I went through the whole experience again, only this time on fast-forward, without the flab and, of course, without being anywhere near as good.

As usual, the whole escapade started out as something else, a childhood dream that was totally unconnected to cricket or, in fact, to reality. As a kid, I loved WWF wrestling. It must have been something about the melodrama of it all that resonated. In particular, I loved this fella called the Undertaker.

If you're not familiar with WWF (or WWE as it's now called), all you need to know is that the Undertaker is absolutely massive, an icon of wrestling, been around for ages. I could add that he's got crazy tattoos and a haircut to match, but that goes with the territory.

After I'd retired from cricket, I had this idea of making a documentary about me becoming a wrestler that ended up with me fighting the Undertaker at the Manchester Arena. Why? I can't quite tell you. One, I'd get fit (a lot of my crazy ideas begin with enforced fitness, which tells you something about my relationship with unenforced fitness). Two, I thought it would be a bit of a laugh.

Sky TV liked the idea. I got into shape and headed off to wrestling school in Tampa, Florida. A car picked up me and Rachael at the airport and took us to this training unit. The first person I saw there was about seven foot tall and almost as wide. 'Are you sure you want to do this?' Rachael asked me. Fair question, but, as usual with me, half an idea had suddenly turned into something I felt committed to. I wouldn't backtrack. I was in it 100 per cent, or that's what I told myself.

The training unit was a little amphitheatre with sixty wrestlers learning the drills. My introduction was four hours of running into people who'd pick me up and then slam me down on my back. Then a break for lunch. Then, for another four hours, I became the slammer rather than the slammed. By this point, I was getting seriously tired. I got into a terrible tangle during one running-jumping-slamming routine and ended up face-planting on to the apron. Day one: broken nose.

The next day was the same routine, only this time I had a back spasm. I went to the physio, whose reaction was, 'Oh, the poor little English boy's got a back spasm!' When he started pushing my back I could feel my ribs separating. I said I thought I'd broken them. 'You can't have done,' he said, 'you'd be in too much pain.' My answer was, 'Well, I want to cry, but I can't in front of all these wrestlers.'

He sent me to a specialist for an X-ray and, sure enough, I had two broken ribs. 'What do you do for a living?' the specialist asked. I explained I was a wrestler. 'How long have you done that for?' he wondered. 'Oh, it's my second day,' I said. He said, 'I suggest you do something else.'

When I got back to the training centre, I showed them the X-rays and suddenly I was accepted, part of the group. But the documentary clearly wasn't going to work. There were too many secrets behind the scenes that they didn't want me to reveal. Instead, they invited me to join the crew of elite wrestlers, to be on the circuit – I'd be fast-tracked on to Royal Rumbles, WrestleMania, all that stuff.

The money was ridiculous. But I didn't really want to run around in my underpants and live in America, so I knocked that idea on the head.

After three days, we went on holiday in Miami for two weeks. I'm really glad, though, about one aspect of the experience. We did an acting class, to practise creating a persona. I had to stand in front of all the other wrestlers, playing the part, provoking them one by one. Acting was one thing I had learnt to do as a cricketer. Acting is part of sport. So I got really into it, laying into these massive men with bulging muscles.


Soon after coming back from Tampa, I bumped into Barry McGuigan, the great ex-featherweight boxing champion. I'd met Barry when making *The Hidden Side of Sport*. One shoot was at a boxing gym and I ended up hitting the pads a few times. 'Do you want to have a proper fight?' Barry asked me when I saw him again. 'Go on, we'll have a fight,' I heard myself saying. I was just winging it, talking off the top of my head. I guess I just swapped the outline of the plan to fight the Undertaker at the Manchester Arena for a professional boxing bout.

Six weeks later, I was in a ring in Essex, boxing against a nineteen-and-a-half-stone half-Nigerian fella to find out if I could take a punch. I'd never boxed at all. I got battered for five rounds. After that, Barry said, 'Yeah, we can do this.' In my head, I was thinking, 'What? Oh no!' But I also felt committed in a weird way. We'd spoken to Sky about a possible fight and they were keen. Once again, there seemed to be a track in front of me and I was just rolling along, only partly in control of what was happening to my own life. (Was I on the rails or off the rails?)

It's true that I've always liked boxing as a sport. Liking it is one thing. Liking it enough to want to get punched? Not so sure about that. So why do it? Yes, there was losing weight and getting some abs and surface issues like that. But there was a much deeper reason, too. I wanted to get the whole professional-sportsman thing out of my system. By the time I retired from cricket, my body had beaten me, it couldn't take any more. At first, the inevitable grieving process for losing a way of life masked something else. Inside I also felt a lot of unfinished business. Whatever I did, there was a hint of emptiness. The itch was still there.

I thought boxing would round everything off, be my last chance to finish that chapter on my terms, close the book and move on. And I'd be able to walk happily away from pro sport and live happily ever after. A lot of sportsmen struggle with the need to be out there competing. You want to escape it, but then you can also persuade yourself that one last time will make everything feel right. It's true for performers in other spheres, too. When they're on the stage they think they'll be happy when they can escape to normal, civilian life. When they're giving normal life a crack, they end up pining for the stage again. You can't take it any more but you can't live without it. It is both a blessing and a curse.

I discovered the problem with boxing very quickly. I didn't like doing it. I enjoyed the fitness training, that was fine. But sparring, that was awful. The whole day was filled with dread. I'd get up and have steak for breakfast (boxers try to lean up with an ultra-high protein diet). Then I'd drive from Surrey, where we were living at the time, to the gym in the East End of London. It's a horrible feeling when you know you're going to get beaten up when you arrive. I've never driven so slowly in my life. It was like *The Green Mile*. The nerves and the fear of going in the ring never left me; it was the same every day. I never knew who I'd be fighting. He could be a seven-foot monster. It was a great feeling afterwards, though, a sense of relief and euphoria. But then the dread would kick back in, knowing that the next day I had to do it all over again.

I had an odd relationship with boxing. I'd had a hard time at school. It was so rough, and being a cricketer made me an easy target – cricket was supposed to be this 'posh' sport. I took plenty of punches but I never punched back. I don't know why not. Instead, I always talked my way out of it. There was a barrier that stopped me hitting back. So now that I found myself in a boxing ring, there was an element of needing to prove myself.

I did find it hard to get my head around some of the conventions of the sport. There is a big thing in boxing about not losing face, about pride. That led me into some tough situations. The second time I sparred, it was with a proper boxer. When he punched me in the face, I thought, 'That's a bit different.' It wasn't just that he was good. He'd also switched gloves to ones with much less padding.

'He's stuffed you there,' said my trainer, Shane McGuigan (Barry's son). 'But you have to stay in now; you can't walk out of the ring.'

My view was different. I'm not so proud that I have to take a beating to prove something to a guy I've just met. But I did stay in the ring. And I got smashed for five or six rounds. The next day was awful, some of the worst headaches of my life. And I had to spar again.

I was committed, I was showing signs of getting better, I was losing weight. But I didn't feel right. Then my great friend Mungo – he was cameraman for the documentary – took me to one side. 'Look, you've got to approach this as acting. When you walk into the gym, play that you're a boxer. It's a role you've got to play.' That struck a chord straight away. Just like cricket. I started stepping into the ring pretending nothing could hurt me, even though inside I was this petrified little boy.

I found out other things about myself, too. I remember the first time I really rocked a man, it was this fella from Barnes, posh lad, rugby player, incredibly fit and pretty tough. I caught him with a right hand and his legs just went. Barry was shouting, 'Finish him! Finish him!' But I couldn't. I just put my arms around him and said, 'Are you all right, mate? Are you OK?'

Think about it. I'd just met the man. Why would you want to punch someone you just met? I had no beef with him. I could never get my head around just punching people. I could never enjoy that or make it feel natural.

I actually enjoyed getting punched more than hitting people. Boxing became like cricket was at the end of my career. I wanted to see how much I could take, how much pain I could absorb. How far could I push myself to get through it? How many times can you hit me and yet I won't go down? Go on, try me. And I'd say to myself, 'You're not going down, you're not going anywhere.' It became perverse. But also not surprising. That contrary streak runs deep in me.

The date for the fight had been fixed for a while. Thousands of people had bought tickets for the Manchester Arena. A week beforehand they found my opponent, the American Richard Dawson. I kept thinking, 'I've got to get out of this. I'm going to embarrass myself, I want to get out.'

I'd boxed myself into a corner. We were living in a flat that had a set of about four stairs. And I'd stand at the top thinking, 'I could do my ankle here, easy. I'm going to put my foot out.' It was like the scene in *Escape to Victory*: please break my arm! Anything to get out of it.

I tried to do it on the stairs. But something wouldn't let me. I just fell on the floor in a heap. When Rachael called out, I yelled back, 'I'm fine, everything's fine.'

As if I wasn't worried enough, I met up with Ricky Hatton a few days before the fight. The previous week he'd lost his comeback fight. I've never seen a man's face as bad in my life. Jesus, I didn't want that to happen to me, to have a face like that on my head. But chatting to Ricky did give me confidence. I needed it – just to get through the press conference before the fight, one of the oddest of my life.

Picture the scene. I'm sitting in the hotel, wearing tracksuit pants and a T-shirt. Barry is on one side of me, the TV commentator Jim Rosenthal is on the other. It's the first time I've ever clapped eyes on big, bad Richard Dawson.

There is a media Q&A for the fighters and one of the English journalists asks Richard, 'So tell us about yourself.'

From this point on, there are two conversations running alongside each other. Dawson is loudly telling the press about himself. And I'm muttering to my trainer Barry, wondering how the hell they picked him as my opponent.

Dawson: 'Oh, I grew up in the American South and I've been shot four times . . .'

Me: 'Er, Barry, this bloke has been shot four times.'

Barry: 'Just roll with it.'

Dawson: 'Yeah, and I've been in prison . . .'

Me: 'Barry, this bloke has been in prison.'

Dawson: 'For GBH . . .'

Me: 'Barry, this bloke has been in prison for GBH! What have you found me here? I thought boxing was all about matching people?'

Dawson: 'And I'm now a debt collector . . .'

Me: 'Barry, this bloke is a debt collector as well. A debt collector who's been shot four times and been to prison for GBH. What's the point of this? What's going on?'

I'm muttering all this under my breath, not fully in control of the words coming out of my mouth. And then it's my turn to be asked a question, my turn to talk about who I am. The best way forward, it seems to me, is a bit of humour.

'I used to play cricket. If you've not seen it, we dress in white and stop for sandwiches every two hours.'

Dawson is looking at me in a rather puzzled way. The room is laughing a bit. Barry is half laughing with me, half trying to stop me.

After the press conference, it is time for the weigh-in. I'm in my underpants in a room full of men with everyone jeering. That already qualifies as a worst-case scenario. But it quickly gets worse. Barry had drilled into me that when two boxers 'face off' at the weigh-in, it's all about point-scoring. 'You've got to stare at him so hard, stare through, stare into his soul.' Barry added that when photographers ask you to turn for photos, you mustn't break your stare. So the done thing is to be the second man to turn, to hold your stare until the other guy has moved.

So I stare into Dawson's eyes. Only I'm not looking at

all hard. And inside I'm just thinking, 'Look away! Look away! Please, look away.' And he does. And then a photographer asks for a photo, and Dawson turns first. And I think, 'Thank God!'

Then I went back to the hotel for the worst night's sleep I've ever had. The kind of sleep where you don't sleep.


Fight day dawns, bringing new anxieties. 'I hope I get through this,' I'm saying to myself. 'I hope I get through this unscathed.' That's my innermost thought. And by the time I'm in the car on my way to the arena, I'm trying to switch on, to get into the zone. Was it like driving to Old Trafford? No it wasn't.

You never know at exactly what time you're going to fight – it depends on the previous bout. When it's between thirty minutes and an hour and a half away, the guys start getting me ready. I get on my undercarriage and my shorts, then they start strapping on my gloves. The referee comes in and signs off my gloves, so now I can't take them off before the fight.

At this point there is time for one more unexpected turn of events. The drug testers arrive, demanding a urine sample. It has to be taken now, apparently. But having a pee wearing taped-up boxing gloves isn't that easy, as you can imagine.

Next thing my brother turns up. He's been drinking and is in high spirits. 'Have you seen the size of him?' That is his helpful question about my opponent. 'He's going to kill you.' I promptly had him kicked out of the dressing room!

Almost immediately, it's time. I put on my Lancashire shirt and step into the corridor, walking into what feels like the unknown. I'd chosen 'Roll With It' by Oasis. The whole place is going off, really going off.

Then I have one of those moments when I step outside myself. I wish I wasn't fighting at all, but in the crowd watching. It's like looking into the stands in the last over of a Test match and wishing I was on the other side of the boundary rope, having a beer with my mates.

Finally I walk into the ring, trying my best to look hard. 'When they announce your name in the ring,' Shane says to me, 'stick your arms out really wide, show him how long your arms are.' I reply that I'm pretty sure he isn't going to be bothered about how long my arms are. But I do it and, of course, I look like a right melon.

I started the fight OK. I knew I could throw straight

shots, but I wasn't very good at cross shots. So I thought I'd hide behind my jab. I'd seen Dawson fight and I knew that if you go after him, he retreats on to his back foot. I just went forward all the time. When he hit me I didn't feel anything. I honestly didn't feel any of his punches. I just kept walking towards him with the crowd singing. It was as if all England was behind me.

And then I got so excited I just started winging it. Mistake. I thought, 'I can take this fella, I can knock him out.' I began windmilling rather than punching properly. I lost all technique. I was a bit embarrassing, in truth.

After the first round, Shane tried to talk to me in the corner but I wasn't listening. I was looking at all my mates in the crowd, watching the scene, soaking it up. So much so that Shane started getting annoyed.

In the second round, after a decent start, I got really excitable. I kept throwing wild punches and missing.

Next thing, out of the blue, I'm facing the wrong way round and I'm on the floor. I didn't even know I'd been hit, I didn't feel a thing. I genuinely thought I'd slipped, I didn't feel anything. That's how high I was on adrenaline. He'd caught me flush on the ear.

It was the first time I'd properly gone down. I didn't know what had happened. I was on the floor and I was looking around and, seeing all my mates around the ring like that, I thought, 'I have to get up.'

So I get up and the ref's going, 'Four, five . . .' And he's got my hand and he says, 'What's your name?' I say, 'What?' He says, 'What's your name?' I say, 'Depends how well you know me. Some people call me Andrew, you know, most people call me Fred . . .' And he starts counting again. So I say, 'Flintoff! Is that what you want?' And he lets me carry on.

After that round I got to the corner and the message was clear: 'Look, you've got two rounds left, you've got to knock him out or win both rounds to win it. Simple as that.'

And I did, winning on points. But I was still angry with myself because I should have knocked him out in thirty seconds. If we're honest, he wasn't very good.

On the other hand, perhaps it was better the way it worked out. I got the full experience. I went into something I didn't know I could do. I got very excited. I was knocked down. I got back up. And I somehow managed to win in pretty unspectacular style. That is a snapshot of my life. So, looking back, I don't really wish it had been neater or prettier.

And I learned plenty. At the press conference afterwards, I explained that I'd wanted to celebrate boxing, to show

how hard it is. But I also knew deep down I wasn't a fighter. So in a way, I got away with it again. I felt embarrassed going to the big party afterwards.

I've seen both sides of boxing. I understand the good it can do. I trained in Monkstown in Ireland. The boxing gym there has turned the community around. The kids all want to fight. So after school, the gym lays out desks and makes them all do half an hour of homework first. Only then can they whack the pads. I guess it's like Dennis's gym in *The Wire*. It has turned kids' lives around. Without boxing they'd be doing bad stuff on street corners.

But there are lots of things about boxing I don't get. I've met some great men in the sport, but also plenty I couldn't relate to at all. All they want to do is talk about hitting people – just like the cricket bores who never stop prattling on about the game. They talk about something else for thirty seconds but then they'll go back to the pleasure of hitting someone. What a horrible way to live. I don't carry that aggression around with me. And I don't want to.

There was only one circumstance in which I found I enjoyed hitting someone: if I thought he wasn't a particularly good human being. One of my sparring partners in London was always mouthing off about this and that.

But he'd never get in the ring. He was always smashing the pads, bragging about having had forty unlicensed fights, then complaining about not being able to get a proper licence. We needed an extra sparring partner one day, so I said, 'Do you fancy it, then?' As usual, he made up a pack of excuses. But I insisted, saying, 'Come on, it'll be fine.' I did enjoy smashing him up, just because of the person he was.

Apart from that, I didn't derive any enjoyment, not from hitting a perfectly nice bloke. When you spar, after hitting each other in the face, you then have a nice little chat. How weird is that?

It's a strange sport to its core. You punch someone until they fall over. But that's not incidental, a bit of collateral damage. It's the whole point. To knock a man out. It's amazing to think that society still considers that to be fine in the twenty-first century. And people are allowed to pay to go and watch it. We don't let dogs fight. We've banned cockfighting. But humans? Yeah, that's absolutely fine.

If you think about the progress of professional sport in general, it has moved away from actual violence towards something more civilised. Tennis is a kind of duel, for example, but there are obviously no actual blows. Yes, there's a tough element to loads of sports. But a sport with the stated aim of knocking someone unconscious?

No other game is anything like that. It's as though boxing is a relic from hundreds of years ago, a link with sport's properly violent past. But I can't help still liking it. Right or wrong, I just like it.

I can think of some cricketers who have boxing instincts in their blood. Harmison, he's got it in him. Ponting, no question. A dark horse you might not expect: Strauss. Boxing also showed me how fitness is so specific to each sport. For the fight, I was definitely fit in the conventional sense of the term. And I looked it. But in bowling terms I was weak. I couldn't have bowled ten overs.

In one important sense, boxing left me more unresolved than ever. The hope was that I'd finally be able to retire the professional sportsman in me, to leave him inside the boxing ring. But even when I was walking out of the Manchester Arena I knew I hadn't achieved that. I'd learned plenty of other things from boxing. But the initial idea – to gain a kind of closure as a professional athlete – backfired.

I woke up the next morning with one idea in my head: 'I've lost all this weight. I've done all this training. I'm going to play cricket again.'

\* \* \*

As usual with me, injury played a hand in things. I'd torn my right shoulder four weeks before the fight. As soon as the fight ended, I couldn't even pick up my right hand. I had a scan the day after the fight. It was bad news. The tendons in my shoulder had to be stitched back on. They fractured the bone to regenerate new growth. The upshot was I was in a sling for three months – my cricket plans had to be put on hold. I couldn't do anything. It was one of my lowest spells, not least because I'd thought all my injuries were behind me.

That said, it wasn't clear I could have played cricket then, even if my shoulder had been 100 per cent. The day after my England retirement in 2009 I'd had surgery on micro fractures in my knee. The knee needed to regenerate, but it didn't work. And then it got to the point where even just walking around in everyday life was awful. We initially went to live in Dubai, but I had to come back to have more surgery.

After the operation, I was on morphine for a week. I've never known pain like it. The doctor had been clear about the prognosis. 'Look, if you have this op, you're never going to run again. And you won't be able to ski.' (Nothing lost there, as I hate skiing.) But he promised me that eventually I'd be able to walk pain-free.

For two years, the pain was terrible. Even now I have

good days and bad days. But the doctor telling me I'd never run was one of those classic challenges. Whenever I'm told I can't do something, my bloody-minded instinct is to show that I can.

Maybe the boxing experience came about from thinking too much like Rocky Balboa. By *Rocky VI*, he's ancient. But he talks about the beast and the animal inside him, how he wants to get it out of him. I could identify with that. There was something in me that wasn't finished. I genuinely thought boxing would release it once and for all, get it out of my system. Instead, that thing was just recast as a hankering to play cricket again. By showing me I could put my mind to something even though I was never going to be that good at it, boxing made the emptiness worse.

I'm like a dog sometimes. If I don't get walked, I get scratchy.

ebrating a great victory in Mumbai by
ng up a happy Andrew Strauss.

As was often the case, something has
amused Steve Harmison and I.

reat way to finish my final Test at Lord's, England win their first Ashes Test there
75 years.

New life, new challenges: canyon rappelling in *Flintoff Versus the World*.

I enjoyed the solitude while making *Alone in the Wild*.

Quite close enough: meeting an elephant in Borneo for *Flintoff Goes Wild*.

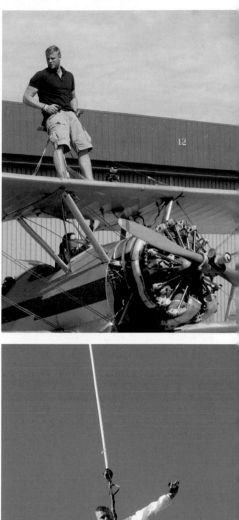

*Above left:* Taking a few tips in Tanzania.

*Above right:* I'm still getting to grips with this, I'm pretty sure I'm not yet in position.

*Below left:* Learning to look like a cowboy for *Flintoff Versus the World*.

*Below right:* Another stunt. This time for *Freddie Flintoff's Record Breakers*.

I think I've seen one of these before somewhere.

Important fact: Goughy chose the outfits.

ky Hatton and Vinnie Jones really opened up to me about depression and mental lth for *The Hidden Side of Sport*.

Having a knock with the great John McEnroe for *A League of Their Own*.

Connecting with my right hand in my professional boxing match.

The whole gym was mesmerised when Mike Tyson popped in.

oting *Special Forces: Ultimate Week of* for the BBC.

King of the Jungle, apparently.

rking hard selling fish and chips on *Lord of the Fries*.

Fun with the boys on set at *A League of Their Own*.

On stage with Clyde Holcroft in my theatre show.

# 11

# BACK TO THE CREASE

Playing cricket again was not part of a grand plan. But after the boxing experience, I couldn't get the idea of giving cricket another go out of my head.

In December 2013 I bumped into Nathan Wood, the former Lancashire player who was coaching at the club's Academy. He asked me to come and help with the young bowlers. So I did. On the day, Nathan asked me to bowl in front of the young lads in the indoor school. Initially, I said I couldn't because my knees wouldn't allow it. Then I bowled just a few and I thought, 'That feels OK, actually. Not too bad.' So I ended up bowling for an hour.

I loved it. Coaching and talking cricket was something I'd missed. I'd been away from that side of my life completely. I found I enjoyed talking about the game again, reconnecting with it. So I went back to the Academy for another session. This time the first-team lads were practising. When I was bowling, I couldn't help thinking, 'Actually, I'm all right at this . . .'

Early in the 2014 season, I started bowling at the first-team lads in the outdoor nets. I could see a few of them looking at me. I was one of the quicker ones, probably the quickest. And then someone mentioned playing for Lancashire again.

There were so many reasons not to go back into cricket. I'd be putting myself out there again. A voice in my head was saying, 'This is boxing all over again. I'm not sure if I can do it. I'm not sure if I even want to do it. There are so many things that could go wrong with this.' Eventually, I arrived at this simple logic: the only 'right' thing is that I want to do it. And I do want to do it. That's a good enough reason for me. I want to do it.

I was concerned about what Rachael would think. She had lived with me as a cricketer and seen what it had done to my body, and to my mind. I knew she didn't want to watch me sitting on the couch for another three months with a busted leg. I knew she didn't want to be the person sitting next to me at the hospital when I woke up after yet another operation.

The kids were more positive. My daughter came out and said, 'You should definitely do this!' I always tell the kids to have a go. And they pick me up if I don't take my own advice.

There was an MCC game scheduled at Lord's against the Rest of the World on 5 July 2014. I really wanted to play in the MCC side so that I could take the field with Sachin Tendulkar. I'd never done that. What a thrill, to play in the same team as Sachin. So straight away I began getting fit and practising for that game.

I spoke to John Stephenson from the MCC about playing in the fixture. John didn't seem keen, saying it was 'only for current players'. That wasn't true, as I knew that Rahul Dravid was certainly playing. John replied, 'I'll see what they say at the committee.' I said, 'Fine, book me in.'

A few weeks later I was in the car with my family when he rang back. I put John on speakerphone. 'Sorry, they don't want you,' John said.

Lord's, Tendulkar, a game I really wanted to play – it was a lot to miss out on. Mike Gatting was picking the team and apparently he wanted a bunch of ageing players from all around the world, but he didn't want me.

As I took this in, my kids were looking at me strangely, asking if I was OK. They had never heard someone say no to me. I put a brave spin on it, 'You know what, it happens. Sometimes you can't have it all your own way.'

Inside I was fuming. I thought, 'Sod you lot, I'm going to play cricket again.' So I said yes to Lancashire. I was back inside the game.

The press reaction was odd. Some journalists seemed to suggest that I'd be 'tarnishing' what I'd achieved before. Hang on a minute. When I retired you said I wasn't very good. Now I'd be undermining my own reputation. That just fuelled the fire. Ian Botham wrote a piece in *The Mirror* saying it was a huge mistake. I'd have preferred it if he'd phoned me up in person and had a chat. Why blow me out in a newspaper? The whole reaction made me want to play even more.

I turned out for my club, St Anne's, on a Saturday afternoon. Bottled it when I was batting, talked myself down the order. I was so nervous. But I got three wickets with the ball. My grandpa was there. I loved it.

I played some Lancashire Second XI fifty-over games. The fielding was desperately boring, torture. How on earth did I manage to get through a whole day of fielding all those times?

My first game back with the First XI was delayed because I sprained my ankle doing a fitness test. And along came the old thoughts: 'I don't know if I'm good enough, perhaps I'm not good enough. But I'm committed now, I can't back down.'

I played my first game in a NatWest T20 Blast match at Worcester in July 2014. It was like my first-class debut all over again. I found out I was playing only about twenty minutes before the start. Chappy told me, my old mate, so that was nice. But it was also very strange. It was what I'd wanted. But when I had it, when it was given back to me, another chance, I wasn't sure I wanted it any more. Instead of feeling happiness, I got really nervous and started to doubt everything. I didn't know what I was doing. I warmed up on autopilot.

Out in the middle, I came on to bowl in the fifth or sixth over – the worst time, as it's the end of the power-play. Back in the day, I'd have been confident about it. The first ball went for four. Third ball disappeared back over my head for six. The crowd, of course, were loving it, shouting at me as I was getting hammered.

After that six, I had a conversation with myself: 'Hang on a minute. You're in a competition. You've not come on as a guest star from TV. You're playing serious cricket here.' From that moment I turned it around a bit and picked up a couple of wickets. The game turned out all right, because we won by fifty runs.

I got a three-for in the next game at Leicester. But

there was an uncertainty about my bowling that I didn't like at all. In the past, there had never been anything tricky or flash about my bowling. My biggest asset was pace and the fact that I knew where the ball was going. Now I didn't have pace and I wasn't 100 per cent sure where the ball would end up.

I used to love bowling at the death in a tight one-dayer or T20. If I had three overs, I knew I could rely on bowling the majority of them as good yorkers. Sixteen yorkers, job done. Now it was a different story. It's one thing running up *knowing* you're going to bowl a yorker. It's great. Running up and *hoping* you bowl a yorker is a completely different experience. An average experience. But we won against Leicester and I came out OK.

Initially, I was all upbeat and buoyant about it. But then I stayed behind in the dressing room after everyone had gone. My fears took over as I convinced myself that I didn't have it any more, that I could no longer do what I wanted out there. I'd found my comeback enjoyable and frustrating in equal measure.

In the middle of all this, I had a TV commitment that had long been agreed. So I went off to the fish-and-chip van to make the *Lord of the Fries* series for Sky TV. I used to get up at six o'clock in the morning before filming to go to the leisure-centre gym at Whitby or wherever we were filming, trying to keep fit. Meanwhile, Lancashire had qualified for the prestigious T20 Finals Day at Edgbaston – both semis and then the final happen on the same day – the showpiece popular event in the English domestic cricket calendar.

Cricket practice? Not that much. All I could manage, between two days' filming, was one trip to Old Trafford for a bowl.

Nonetheless, I met up with the team and travelled down to Birmingham. I was never going to play really; I accepted that. Then suddenly in the nets, I don't know what happened. I started quick, probably bowling mid-80s, which was faster than everyone else. I could see the rest of the team looking at me. It was nice to think that they all thought I still had it. But I didn't think I had. Anyway, the other lads had got Lancashire to the Finals. I couldn't just waltz in and play.

I was all over the place mentally. I was flattered that they wanted me in the squad. And I was disappointed not to be in the starting XI. I had all the voices in my head. All in all? Though part of me was disappointed that the skipper, Paul Horton, hadn't picked me, the greater part of me was relieved that he wasn't chucking me out there.

So I did the twelfth-man duties in the semi-final. And then, right at the end of the semi, Kabir Ali fell on his shoulder. He was obviously knackered, gone. And the message was relayed to me: 'You're playing. Go and get ready.' I thought, 'Bloody hell, I've got to play in the final here.' It was exactly five years after I'd retired in 2009.

There was only a twenty-minute turnaround before it started, so I ran round the side of the ground to the dressing room. We bowled first. It was a full house at Birmingham, and in the early stages I felt like a spectator. Usually when professional sportsmen say, 'I felt like a spectator', they mean, 'I didn't think I was making a positive contribution to the team effort.' I mean it literally.

I was looking at the pitch with the crowd, I was part of the crowd, and I was thinking to myself, 'How has this happened? What's going on? I was selling chips two days ago in Whitby on Sky TV and now I'm in the final at Edgbaston playing for Lancashire in front of 20,000 people. What's going on?'

I had that nervous laughter. Bumble was waving at me from the commentary box and Vaughany was messing about. I had to avoid getting involved in all that. I just couldn't register that the match had begun. Finally, I said very consciously, 'You're in a final, get a grip of yourself.'

I came on to bowl. At the top of my mark I was thinking, 'Here goes.' And I got Ian Bell out first ball. I was nowhere near as fast as in the nets. I think I'd seized up a bit. Just as well. Belly middled it, but because the ball was a bit slower than he'd expected, he chipped it in the air to Karl Brown running back from mid-on.

I stood there with my arms stuck out in that silly way. I didn't know what else to do. I've got my arms out, I've done this before, this works. They like this, don't they? This is what they want. In my head: 'I don't know what's going on here. I've got Ian Bell out first ball. Am I getting away with this, too?'

The first over went well, tight and with that important wicket. I didn't want to see the speed gun because I doubted I was breaking 80. In the second over, I bowled the worst ball of my life. This right-handed lad had smashed Jimmy Anderson the over before. He seemed to back off to give himself room and whop it over square leg. Sometimes when I'm bowling, it's not a conscious thing: I can see the batsman playing a certain style, something clicks in my subconscious and I adapt. It's not planned; it just happens. So as I ran up, I saw him backing away and I followed him. I saw him go, bowled it – and,

God, it was above waist height. He just plonked it out of the ground for six. And it was a no-ball. The free hit went for another six. Back down to earth.

I was livid at one point near the end. I'd bowled two overs for 20. But most of that was because of that one ball. So apart from that it had been decent. But there we were, getting smashed at the death. I said to Jos Buttler, 'I should be bowling now.' More than anything, I was upset with myself. When I was in my prime, Tom Smith would never have bowled that final over. I'd have grabbed the ball and stood at the end of the mark and just said to the skipper, 'I'm bowling, deal with it.' The sort of thing I said to Straussy at Lord's in 2009. I should have just told Paul Horton, 'Off you go, I'll handle this.' But I didn't.

For me, that's hiding. I hid. I cursed myself. I scarcely ever had that feeling of hiding in my whole career. Warwickshire ended up getting 181.

I was down to bat at nine. Nine? I did protest about number nine. I always distrusted players who complained about being hard done by but were reluctant to put themselves out there. So I put my hand up when we kept missing the big shots: Just send me in now. I'll swing from ball one. I'm batting nine, there's nothing to lose, send me in.'

They didn't. I ended up going in when we needed 30 off thirteen balls. First ball, let's push for one, off the mark. And then I was facing Oliver Hannon-Dalby, tall gangly kid who'd just got a wicket. With two balls left in the over, I hit him for six over long-off. Next ball, another six.

We were back in the game. At this point my eyes had gone; they had that out-of-control look. But I remember standing in the middle of the pitch, thinking: 'This is where I should be. This is it. I'm not a commentator. I'm not a spectator. I'm not a captain on *A League of Their Own*. I'm not anything apart from a cricketer. That's what I am. That's what I do.' It was the first time I'd felt that since retiring. I'd missed it.

After I'd hit Hannon-Dalby for six, he gave me that smile people put on to tell you they're not bothered. He was looking down at me and smiling as if it was my first game. I gave him a serve, shouting at him, 'What the fuck are you smiling at, you big -----?' I got totally carried away. Embarrassing. I apologised to him straight after the game.

[Quick aside: I've got little time for sledging. I've done it a few times and I still feel wrong about it. I've said and done things I'm embarrassed about. Very embarrassed about. I don't mind a bit of chat when it's funny. But straightforward abuse? I don't think that's right. And I don't subscribe to the view that there's a complete separation between on and off the field. Bit convenient that, isn't it? You wouldn't walk into someone's office and abuse him and then say on the way out, 'Let's go and have a pint together now . . .' That's why I like rugby referees. They don't stand for it. Nigel Owens. Brilliant. When the England captain Chris Robshaw came up to complain about a decision, he just waved him off: 'No, Christopher, go away.' He says things like 'Carry on like this and you won't last the eighty minutes.' It's brilliant. I only wish football was like that.]

Fourteen were needed off the last over, to be bowled by Chris Woakes. We scrambled a bye to get me back on strike. Thirteen off five. I really should have nailed the next one. In the slot, I aimed for extra cover, but scooped it over mid-off – two runs. Eleven off four. Ball three, I went right back into my crease and got another two, this time through midwicket. Nine off three. Boundary needed. I should have gone across my stumps and whipped it. Instead, I bunted down the ground and I couldn't get back for the second run.

I'd left Steve Parry with far too much to do: eight off

two balls. He managed a two and a single. It was over. We'd lost.

Coming off the field was strange, disorientating. I knew I should have won that game: I shouldn't have bowled that crap ball and I should have got those runs.

I still play out those few balls in my mind. It keeps me awake at night, not whipping that yorker to the boundary. I saw Woakes the following winter and told him what I should have done.

But the worst thing about it was it wasn't so much the losing, it was that the game had ended. I was loving it. I was out in the middle at Edgbaston, somewhere I'd loved playing in my prime. It was just how it should be, how it used to be. Lost in playing cricket. I wanted that game to keep going on and on, wanted to bat longer, to hold the moment, to stay in the experience.


After that Finals Day, I was given the opportunity to play T20 for Brisbane in the 2014–15 Big Bash. Again, so many reasons not to. But the overriding factor was that I wanted to do it and I'd never have the chance again.

I didn't embarrass myself exactly, but I found the bowling hard. I was in so much pain. The batting I found easy. Loved it. No thigh pads, nothing, just watching the ball, no fear. I think, after the boxing, fear has gone. I got 40 in one game, against the Sydney Sixers. I wouldn't say it was the best I've ever played, but it convinced me I had reached a different level of maturity as a batsman.

The interesting thing about that innings was that I was commentating while I was batting – one of the features of the Big Bash. When the technician came into the dressing room and said, 'You're commentating today,' I had all my usual excuses ready, the ones I'd used earlier in the tournament. Then I thought, 'No more excuses. I'll do it.'

It was strangely liberating. Once I started walking out to the middle, Adam Gilchrist in the commentary box began firing questions into my earpiece. So I forgot to be nervous, in effect. I was too busy chatting with Adam. I just batted, without a care in the world.

Another commentator that day was Viv Richards. How cool is that? Batting in the middle in a T20 while chatting with Viv up in the commentary box – amazing.

My only regret about the Big Bash is that I wish I'd played better. It was Stuart Law, my old Lancashire teammate, who had signed me as coach. If only I could have repaid him with some stronger performances. When he lost his job, I felt my failures certainly hadn't helped his cause.

From my perspective, I could see how much I'd learned in my time away from the game. If I'd been fit to play properly, I had the mindset to do really well. If only I'd had that carefree attitude during that disastrous trip to Australia in 2006–07.

That's one of the oddities of sport. In most other professions – if you're a surgeon or an author or whatever – once you get a bit of life experience, when you're in your mid to late forties, that's when you're emotionally ready, and that's typically when you take on the big challenges. In sport, you are thrust into big time in your mid twenties. Emotionally, you're just a kid. I wasn't mature enough to take it on. If I was able to play cricket now, I'd be so much better. So that was frustrating.

The nice thing is that the feelings I wanted to get out of my system – towards the game and towards sport – they've all gone. I was lucky enough to get the chance to play again for the very reason I started in the first place: because I enjoyed it. But it's gone now, both the aptitude and the urge. I don't catch myself thinking, 'I want to play again.'

When I retired first time around, injury had beaten me, and I hated that. This time I've realised I'm no longer good enough. And I can handle that. It's fine that I'm not good enough. I can walk away now. I'll get my cricket fix playing for St Anne's on the odd Saturday afternoon.

I tasted the game at the top level one last time. So I'm good, I'm done.


A couple of things came out of playing professional sport again.

First, I enjoyed just being around cricket. And that's stayed with me. I don't want to lose the passion I feel for cricket again; I'd definitely lost it for a while. Now I'm going to cherish it. I love taking my boys to Old Trafford. I'd missed the community, just chatting about cricket. The other day I caught up with Straussy and really enjoyed the conversation. When we played together, I probably didn't appreciate just how much I liked him and enjoyed his company.

You forget the strength of the relationships you build. And once you've left the set-up, everyone moves on so fast. The phone stops going, you don't get invited to this wedding, you don't get invited to that christening. That was hard to take when I first left cricket. Whereas now, it's all good.

Secondly, I've come to see how important routine is to me. All through my cricket career I used to ruck up about discipline and being on time. Must have driven people mad. I pushed my luck, often just for the sake of it. I resisted a pattern to my life.

When it's all gone, you begin to see how much it matters. That's why the boxing was the best thing. It focused my mind again. Even though I didn't enjoy the actual boxing at all, I proved to myself that I could get into something again. Routine, discipline, consistency. I'm still reaping the benefits of boxing today.

## 12

# A PATIO IN THE JUNGLE

APPEARING on the first series of the Australian version of *I'm a Celebrity . . . Get Me Out of Here* in 2015 was a shot to nothing. If my time in the jungle went well, it would help my work in Australia. If it went really badly, I just wouldn't go back. No big deal.

Beforehand, I didn't particularly want to do the show. I wasn't desperate to have a reality show on my CV. They first asked me when I was playing the Big Bash. I had seen trailers for the show. 'No way,' was my initial response.

When I got back home, the requests kept on coming and I kept on stalling. One Friday evening, the organisers said I had to decide by the following Monday. I'd asked a few people for an opinion. I was struck that no one said, 'No, don't do it.' So I'd run out of excuses apart from stubbornness.

On the Saturday night, I was appearing on *The Jonathan*

*Ross Show*. While I was filming it, Rachael agreed on my behalf that I would go on *I'm a Celebrity*. In the end, it was good that she made the decision for me. It was all pretty quick. Before I knew it, I was on a plane heading to South Africa (which is where they record the Australian version, obviously).

I didn't find the flight easy, to be honest. People would say, 'Where are you going?' And I'd reply, 'Oh, just going to the Kruger Park to do a bit of work.' The next question would be 'Oh, what kind of work are you doing over there?' 'Just going to see a few animals . . .' I'd say, trailing off lamely. The air hostesses were asking, 'Where are you off to? Going for a nice break?' Throughout the flight I couldn't bring myself to tell anyone I was doing reality TV.

I got off the plane in Joburg and someone met me to make sure I got my connecting flight. That was just as well because I was getting myself into a flap. But this fella would not leave me alone. When I went out for a fag he stood next to me. All the time I was thinking, 'I don't want to do this, I really don't want to do this.'

I waited three hours for the internal flight, with this chap next to me, and we scarcely spoke. In my mind, I kept saying, 'This is a mistake, I shouldn't do this, I'm going home.'

On the flight to the Kruger Park I was equally withdrawn and keen to avoid conversation. In the next seat was a bouncy American lady, about fifty years old, wearing a jumper with 'Minnesota' written all over it. I could see it coming. She cheerfully launched in: 'Hey, hey, where are you from?' I said, 'Preston.' She replied, 'I'm Minnesota, born and raised.' I didn't ask. I wasn't interested. So I put my head back down.

After touching down, a bad day got even worse. I was driven up to a holding house where I was to do the press photographs and the pre-show interviews. This element was all staged, still wearing our own normal clothes. They'd say, 'Look scared!' And I'd say, 'Nope. This is what you're getting. This is it.' Then they'd say, 'Can you just kneel down and pretend there's an animal to your right and you don't like it?' 'No.' 'OK, there's a meerkat to your left!' 'But there isn't. Can we just get on with this?'

I sensed a bit of an atmosphere in the room. Then they asked us to put the gear on, what we'd be wearing in the jungle, the red trousers and the hat. It didn't fit, not at all. It was all too tight. So I said, 'I'm not wearing that, I'll go in my own clothes.' 'You can't go in your own clothes.' 'It's too ------- tight. I can't spend a month in these, they're choking me, not happening.'

In the end the seamstress made them bigger and I got changed. As soon as I put on the uniform, there was an instant change – in how I felt and in their attitude towards me. I felt like a prisoner. Instead of being asked to do things nicely and politely, I was just getting told what to do. Inside my head, I was thinking, 'What's just happened here?' I nearly pulled the pin there and then.

They put me in the back of a van with blacked-out windows, bin liners around the windows, so I wouldn't know where I was going. I'd done a little planning. I'd bought some sleeping tablets from Boots and taped them inside my Akubra hat.

I'd seen enough of the English version of *I'm a Celebrity* to know that they never take you straight to camp, there's always a twist at the beginning. So I wasn't too surprised by what happened next. When I arrived there was a sign on the floor which I stopped to read. As I was reading it, a big net full of leaves was pulled up around me and I was hoisted halfway up a tree.

So for about ten minutes I was just dangling in this net. Then we were led off to a cave. It was St Valentine's day, and I spent the night in a cave with another contestant, Julie Goodwin, a chef. She was lovely. But I felt really bad because she was so excited – for her, this was amazing – while I was just nonplussed.

The next morning it was off to join the eight others in the camp. And Merv Hughes was there! It was like, 'Thank God for that, Merv's here.'

Merv is an amazing man. I used to love watching him as a cricketer. He's someone you're drawn towards. He wasn't particularly good, but talk about a 'personality player' – he epitomised that. He bowled on character as much as ability. The crowd loved him, even when they paid him the backhanded compliment of getting stuck into him.

In the jungle, Merv enjoyed expressing his rare talent for farting. He'd just sit there and let rip, really deep-pitched and loud farts. I laughed every time. But this lad Joel Creasey, a comedian, was horrified. Merv never wore his shirt, so his hairy back was permanently on display. Eventually, he won everyone over. For all his faults, he worked harder than anyone. And if anybody had a problem, Merv would be the one to sort it out. Every night just before sleep I'd look over at Merv and he'd mouth, 'You all right?' He's a real carer. Lovely man. I wish he'd won it, really.

When Merv got voted off, it was a bit of stitch-up. We were talking about Mark 'Chopper' Read, the notorious Australian gangster and murderer. (Bizarrely, the cricketer Craig White's dad used to be his prison guard.) We were all doing impressions and Merv was impersonating this Chopper Read. With Merv in mid-Chopper mode, somebody in the camp asked him to get something and Merv replied, 'Get it yourself or I'll chop your head off!' He was still in character, pretending to be Chopper Read. But they played the clip on TV out of context. That was the end of Merv; he was booted out.

The rest of them, I didn't know any of them, never seen them before. It felt like gate-crashing the worst party ever. Everyone was hungry, everyone was whingeing. There was this girl called Anna Heinrich, who'd apparently starred in a show called *The Bachelor* or something, and she just stood in front of me fluttering her eyelids. What was she doing?

So I just sat on my bed for the first two days watching these strangers, wondering what I'd got myself into. But then I started to get my head around it and after a while it dawned on me. Sitting on a bed . . . sleeping twelve or fourteen hours a night . . . no need to say anything unless I was confident that it would make the edit and get into the programme . . . not too much idle chitchat . . . just the occasional interjection to wind them up – it was the easiest thing I'd ever done.

Call that work? I was on a set contract for the first two weeks, with a guaranteed figure, and then after that I was on a day rate. So when the two weeks were up I started trying. I was like, 'Right, hang on a minute, if I stay here until Friday, that'll pay for the kids' bathrooms. If I stay in over the weekend, that'll do the patio out the back.' Every day I had a goal. I'd go to bed at night thinking, 'Happy days, that's the kitchen covered.'

That was how I rationalised the jungle experience to myself. I did nothing. And even the trials and ordeals, if you had fun with them, they were fine. I ate scorpions, cockroaches and all sorts. Getting whatever it is in your mouth is the tricky bit. Once you've done that, it's easy. Crunch.

It was ridiculous the way some people complained about the food: 'I'm starving, oh, I'm starving!' Well, no, you're not starving. You definitely will not starve. Trust me. This is a TV programme. They are not going to let you die. They will feed us.

I had breakfast in bed every morning. Never got up once for breakfast. Each day I'd wake up and there'd be a pot of porridge on the end of my bed, perfect. At night it was rice and beans, which is not too bad.

I even got frustrated at one point because some of the others were getting so cranky about being hungry that the programme-makers caved in and started giving us extra. Why? In the 'talk room', I told the organisers they were missing out on prime entertainment. 'What are you doing?' I said. 'Why are you feeding them? You're about forty-eight hours away from absolute carnage here. You're making a mistake. It's just about to go off. You've got them. It'll be brilliant.' But apparently on Australian TV they don't like it to get too spicy. They don't like shows that have too much direct confrontation.

Other contestants would say, 'How can they speak to us like this? How can they treat me like this? I'm a big deal in Australia.' That kind of chat was the worst part. You could see people's bizarre relationship with 'fame', if that's the right word, their hunger for celebrity.

One activity in the camp was a game about Twitter. A tweet was read out to us and we had to guess who the tweet was about. For some of the contestants it was the highlight of their week, a snippet of feedback from the outside world saying, 'You're amazing, you're the best TV personality ever . . .' And they'd be like, 'Oh, that's me!' But then it wouldn't be them at all. Sad, really.

Meanwhile, I was still doing nothing. Absolutely nothing. Well, except sleeping, for which I have a real aptitude, especially now the medication I'm on includes a sleeping agent. So at night, I'm just gone, lovely.

I got on really well with one of the hosts, Chris Brown. He's a vet as well as a TV presenter. He's like Mr Perfect. If you could draw the perfect man – square jaw, chiselled – it'd be him. I never planned on doing it, but I used to tease him for being too perfect. That's one of the reasons I won, I think. It became a running joke. They cut a lot out, of course. But the morning segment, when the presenters come into the camp, is live on TV. So he had nowhere to escape at that point. I'd hammer him. There'd be a pause as he waited for something clever to be piped into his earpiece. And then the producer would feed him a line and he'd come back at me.

The nicest part of the experience was after about three weeks, when people dropped their guard and you had some decent conversations. The difficulty for some of them, however, was that they weren't comfortable in their own skin, so they found it hard to allow themselves to behave 'normally'.

Total experience? I thought it was all right. Occasionally

funny, never difficult. I didn't mind it. I'm not especially proud of having won. But I am proud of the fact that I raised £100,000 for Glenn McGrath's charity. We all had to nominate an Australian charity and I went for Glenn's, which he set up when his first wife died from cancer.

But I wouldn't want to gloss over my own motives. There was definitely a mercenary side. Other contestants would do increasingly stupid things to try to make the edit and I was prepared to make the odd gesture, too. I shaved my hair because an eviction vote was looming. I'll sacrifice my hair for a new bathroom; it's fine.

I signed up to the jungle because I had a month where I wasn't busy and I had the time. I would never have got paid that well for a month's work anywhere else. My dad worked his nuts off, day in, day out, doing a proper job. Eventually, I couldn't rationalise turning down that amount of money just because I was too scared of eating an insect.

Ironically, I think viewers appreciated the honesty. I wasn't going on a 'journey'. I wasn't going to 'find myself'. I was just sitting there working and, as it turned out, winning.

\* \* \*

In the jungle we carved a chessboard on a tree stump. It was funny because I really wanted to play, but I couldn't handle the thought of losing. An ex-professional sportsman admitting he is competitive may not sound surprising. But it's probably not the first association people make with me – they'd say I was laid-back. Instead of the popular perception that I'm ultra-confident but not that competitive, the truth is probably the other way around: I'm not that confident but I am ultra-competitive.

I've always tried to hide my competitiveness because I'm a bit ashamed of it. It's still there. I often shied away from competition because I hated losing so much. While competitiveness can bring out the best in me, it has also brought out the worst.

My schoolboy chess came in handy in the dressing room at Lancashire. They were surprised at my interest at first. On the bus one day the senior lads were playing and I acted dumb: 'What's all this chess about, then?' So I took on Athers and beat him. It was like taking candy from a baby.

I won a chess tournament in Preston once, and I should never have won it. There were far better players than me. But I got on a roll and then I just couldn't lose. And that was very similar to my cricket. Things would just start to happen and go my way.

I tell myself all the time that I'm not competitive. And I tell other people I'm not competitive. But I am. If I lose, I'll put this face on and say I'm happy for someone. I'll give the impression that I'm not bothered. I'll mask it – probably a defence mechanism. But deep down, I find losing difficult.

That really bothers me. It's almost self-indulgent, isn't it? Why do I need that? Why do I need to win everything I enter? Why can't I be happy for other people? Am I that shallow? I can't be happy for someone beating me? No, I can't. I really can't. It's horrible.

In the jungle, I tried talking myself out of wanting to win. I'd say, 'She deserves to win, because she's had it tougher than me.' But deep down, I probably did want to win. And that was only reality TV! Apart from the money, for me and for the charity, it was pointless. So I was embarrassed at myself for having that secret desire to win. Talking myself out of something while also wanting it – that's really strange. Everything seems to be a competition, everything.

That competitiveness intersects with the performer. I couldn't really box, but at the end of it I got some real satisfaction from doing something that other people didn't expect, and that I didn't expect.

It's like risk and reward. Sitting around doing things I know I can do – I get no satisfaction from that. The result is that I put myself under a lot of pressure. With something like the 2015 theatre tour – my two-handed show with Clyde Holcroft – I'll just commit and then hope I can make it work. Even when I went to watch at the Comedy Store the other night, there was a spare slot and I said, 'Tell them I'll do it.'

It's not that I think I can turn my hand to anything, not at all. I'm probably due a massive fall soon. Though I am fearful of my reaction when I discover things I can't do. My reaction to not being able to play cricket again was terrible.

Putting myself into situations I don't know I can get through has become a habit. More an addiction. And I've got a very addictive personality.

The worst thing about the addiction is that if you do something well, you become the centre of attention. It would be much nicer if I could just do it and then move on. If I do win or succeed at something, I feel a bit embarrassed for winning, then as soon as the embarrassment goes, it is instantly replaced by self-criticism. The worst of both worlds.

I start thinking, 'I could have done better. I should have

done better.' It's a never-ending cycle. In cricket, I can tell you about my bad days in a lot more detail than the good ones.

I've become a host on an Australian TV show called *The Project*, which is the equivalent of our *One Show*. It's interesting that an opportunity like that should come in Australia and not in England. I'm not sure why that is.

It's an attractive idea, spending a portion of each year in Oz. It's sunny, for starters. The boys could just play cricket all year round. But it's more complex with girls, isn't it? There's a different dynamic. They have 'friendship groups' and things. I never had a sister, so it's all new to me. Tell you what, I've always thought they'd be the best sledgers, teenage girls. They'd get right stuck in; they have a natural gift for what Steve Waugh called 'mental disintegration': 'Oh, look at you. Have you put a bit of weight on? One jean size up at least!'

Presenting *The Project* has led to some odd experiences already. I recently interviewed Mark Wahlberg. That was a disappointment. He'd made a film called *Ted 2* about a teddy bear. It was a press junket in a fancy London hotel, with twenty-five journalists waiting for their precious time slot with 'the star'. I pity the poor folk who came later in the day. He was bad enough at the start.

Terrible film, *Ted 2*. Sitting through it once was more than enough. Can't imagine how awful it must have been making it. He looked a bit haggard sitting there promoting a film he didn't want to talk about. It was like getting blood out of a stone. Wahlberg's probably got a big house. It's where your priorities lie. I pitied him, really.

I had four minutes. My thoughts were, 'If you don't want to talk about it, that's fine by me.' There was a girl at the back of the room looking at me and miming the countdown: 'Three minutes! . . . Two minutes!' After two and a half minutes I said, 'I've had enough now,' stood up and walked out.

In recent times, I've found myself talking the truth more and more. Maybe that's one of the things that's working in my favour. Afterwards, when the other interviewers said, 'How did that go?' I said, 'It was dreadful. He's not interested, is he? It was pointless.' It was like something had been lifted off their shoulders and all these young journalists who had been pretending he was great suddenly admitted, 'Yeah, he was like that with me.'

Also for *The Project*, I went to see Amanda Seyfried, the American actress who starred in *Mamma Mia*. On a separate occasion, I've actually sat with her on a TV couch for three hours. Not that she had any idea. So I spent the first ten minutes talking to the cameramen, because I've worked with them before and they're good lads. Meanwhile, she's sat on the chair waiting for her questions. And then the woman who was running it said urgently, 'But you've only got two minutes left, would you like to speak to Amanda?' And I said, 'Oh, go on then.'

She has famously big eyes. In her new film she gets repeatedly referred to as 'Gollum', after the character in *The Lord of the Rings*. So I mentioned that to her and she wasn't having it at all. 'I've got big eyes,' she said. 'I don't find it funny.' Comedy.

# 13

# ENGLAND TODAY

Tʜɪs England team excites me. Look at the England side now and it contains some of the best players we've ever had. The captain has just gone past the all-time run-scoring record. Ian Bell's got twenty-plus hundreds. Joe Root is going to be brilliant. England's best ever bowler, James Anderson, is playing. Stuart Broad has got 300 Test wickets.

So I was baffled by a lot of the negativity of the analysis about English cricket. It annoys me. When I listen to the pundits I find myself thinking, 'I played with a lot of these guys. Watched the others. And they were OK. Some of them weren't the most thrilling players, if we're honest. And now they are pulling apart today's team as though the game were easy.'

Don't they remember what it's like to be out there? Honestly, it baffles me. They seem to have forgotten how it felt when they were playing badly. When you watch cricket after you've retired, you've got to constantly remind yourself how hard it was. I occasionally catch myself thinking I could do this or that. But then you remember what it was like to walk out at Lord's, shockingly out of nick. It was very, very difficult.

It's completely different in Australia. Perhaps it's the background of winning and being successful over so many years. People who are comfortable in themselves and what they've done don't feel the need to take a cheap swipe at others. The pundits there just want Australia to carry on that tradition of winning. Sometimes I sense the opposite situation in England, as though the ex-players who didn't win anything are only too keen to get stuck into the next generation.

I find it amazing how grudging many pundits have been towards Alastair Cook. Really disappointing. He's made 9,000 runs and it's almost as if they can't rustle up a decent adjective. He's scored all those runs and yet every time he walks out to bat you'd think he was playing for his career. If you have a ten-year career, as he has, there is always going to be a lean patch. But his bad spells are better than most people's purple patches.

Alastair Cook has been totally vindicated. I just didn't understand the critical angle. All common sense said he was going to come good. Why was everyone on his back? Here is someone who's scored more runs than any other Englishman, more hundreds, and he's got them against the best teams. And when he finally went through a little bit of a rocky patch, everyone turned on him. He was always comes going to come good. As a batter, he's going to end up almost like Tendulkar. Even then he won't be good enough for his critics!

I've enjoyed Cook scoring runs again. I loved it when he lifted the Ashes. I'm not one for crying and over-egging stuff, but it was nice when he got emotional after winning the Ashes. You saw what it meant to him.

Cook isn't a natural orator. So what? It doesn't matter. He's got the backing of the team; that's obvious. And if you've got that, you don't have to make the right decisions all the time. He's a solid lad. Just let him get on with it. In 2014, there was a big push to get him sacked as captain. It didn't work. Some people still keep niggling away, questioning him.

In terms of batsmanship, the idea that Alastair Cook can't do this and can't do that makes me laugh. Coming up to thirty Test hundreds as a thirty-year-old? Wow, amazing. And yet the pundits say he can't hit an off-drive? Let me repeat: almost thirty hundreds aged thirty! He could end up scoring more Test runs than Tendulkar.

What will the critics say then? That he was OK off his legs? That bowlers somehow never worked out how to bowl at him, even after twenty years? It's ridiculous. Come out and say it: what he has done is already extraordinary. And there's much more to come.

I can't take much credit for my captaincy, but I did insist Cook should make his debut in India in 2006. Duncan Fletcher wanted to promote Matt Prior to open. I put my foot down. Cook was there as cover, to open the batting if required. So why were we talking about Prior?

I had scarcely seen Cook play at that stage. But I liked his manner and his calmness around the team. There was just something about him. It was probably the best decision I ever made as a captain. Cook got a hundred on debut and he was off.

Some people seem to think mental toughness is about mouthing off or staring players down. Not at all. It's about playing the next ball as well as you can. That's the only ball that matters. Just watch Cook for a lesson in how it's done.

I am very optimistic about England's current group of players. At the start of this season, however, England did have one massive stroke of good fortune. They played against New Zealand. Usually luck implies your opponents were rubbish. Not this time. New Zealand were terrific: attacking, fearless, well led. The way Brendon McCullum talks cricket and plays cricket is brilliant for the game.

It rubbed off on England. England went toe to toe and matched them. Even if England had tried to play dour cricket, I'm not sure they could have kept it up in that environment. New Zealand's sense of adventure proved infectious. They were the perfect team for England to play after the desperate low of the World Cup.

It's one thing to say, 'We're going to play with no fear.' Talking the talk is easy. But doing it is completely different. Who had the guts to carry it through? Guys like Joe Root and Ben Stokes are really doing that now.

I like the look of Stokes. I usually have no interest in comparing new players with myself, but there are some interesting parallels here. He is more classical than me. He's a proper batsman. He doesn't have to manufacture scoring opportunities – which I had to do sometimes – they just happen. His batting will end up stronger than his bowling.

Cricketers have moments when everything falls into place and you realise how you want to play. It doesn't necessarily happen the first time you succeed. I got a hundred in New Zealand in 2002, but things only really clicked after two knocks against South Africa in 2003 – the 142 at Lord's and then the 95 at The Oval. Your first hundred isn't necessarily the real turning point.

With Stokes, though he played superbly in 2013 for a hundred at Perth in his second Test, his 98 and 101 in the first Test at Lord's against New Zealand may prove the real breakthrough. He played some extra-cover drives, great shots rather than 'big' shots, where you just thought, 'Wow!' After my hundred at Lord's I suddenly felt at home and my mindset changed when I went out to bat. I'd say the same thing has happened with Stokes.

We are different when it comes to bowling. My strengths were limited. But because of those limitations, I had to nail down the things I could do. I could bowl a length, I could bowl a yorker, I could bowl a bouncer. I could bowl around the wicket. That was pretty much it. I knew where every ball was going. If it was reverse-swinging, I might exploit that too. Above all, however, I used aggression and bravado.

Stokes can actually do a lot of things. He's got all the skills – swing, pace, movement. Yet he's a bit of an enigma, because although he's quite tall, he doesn't bowl like a big lad. I don't know if it's because his action is a bit tight and restricted. He also could have more presence.

He creates an aura when he bats. He should work on the same quality, the same manner, when he bowls.

With Stokes, there seems to be an animal in him that they don't want to let out. Damn it, just let it out. That's one of the things that's great about him. He's like one of the Free Folk in *Game of Thrones*, 'beyond the Wall'. Northern, ginger, a bit rough and aggressive-looking. Wind him up and just let him go.

I spoke to Stokes briefly during the Big Bash. He can bowl at 90 mph and I think bowling fast is the way forward for him. He should run in and bowl quick, not within himself in the early to mid 80s. If he can do that, because he is also a genuine batsman, he will become a very precious player for his captain, his team and his country.

His bowling will naturally improve technically. Look at any bowler from their first game to their last. Very few don't evolve and improve. Jimmy Anderson now is different from the 2003 bowler. I changed and tightened up, too. I was a lot more slingy at the beginning, relying more on strength than rhythm. Over time I got taller at the crease. That's not down to coaching. You've got to figure it out for yourself. The quicker you do it, the longer your Test career will be.

I think Mark Wood will do exactly that. He's going to

be a good Test bowler. He's like a raw version of Simon Jones. At the moment, everything is a bit rushed and he collapses a little at the crease. But as he plays and gains confidence, it will all come. I played against him once in a benefit game. I was meant to bat at the top of the order, but I had a look at Wood bowling at 90-odd miles an hour and I sent in Michael Vaughan instead!

Above all, Wood brings something fresh and different to the bowling side. He adds an extra dimension and livens it up. Partly that's his character. He is a natural and unaffected lad from Ashington in Northumberland. Secondly, his technique has a useful homespun quality. These days, there's a tendency for bowling to become very samey. Yet we know that many of the great bowlers – like Malinga and Jeff Thomson – are different. There is always plenty of room for people like Wood who can offer a surprise tactic.

One area that may still need attention for this England team is control with the ball. Who is going to bowl the overs and hold down one end while the attacking bowlers rest and recover? The 2005 Ashes team had Ashley Giles. It can't be said enough that Gilo was one of the most important players of that period, because he could bowl thirty overs, even in the first innings when it wasn't turning, and he'd be tight, going for one and a half or two runs an over. He was a massive help to the quick bowlers.

This England team doesn't seem to be getting that from their spinner. I'm not inclined to blame Moeen Ali, though, because it is extremely difficult for any off-spinner to do that job. If you're a mystery off-spinner (like Saqlain or Murali), then fine. But if you're just an off-spinner, it's very hard to supply consistent control for the captain.

Who could fill that role among the seamers? Anderson is a classic new-ball bowler; Broad is a form bowler, who can be unstoppable when he gets on a roll – just look at his remarkable 8–15 that helped regain the Ashes; Wood is more of a surprise package; Stokes is raw. Not easy to see the answer there.

Someone who could perform that holding role – if the team changes – is Chris Woakes. When he gets it right, he is like a quicker version of Matthew Hoggard. He could do that job for this England team.


Where English cricket can improve is in the way it sells the sport. One of the things I love about cricket is that you can identify with the people who are playing. I love going to Old Trafford now to watch Lancashire. Even as a professional, I always felt that if I hadn't been playing on the pitch, I'd have been sitting in the crowd watching. There shouldn't be too much distance between players and fans. We are part of the same game and that is much more important than players learning to say the 'right' thing.

At times in recent years I've sensed the gap between players and fans widening, especially in English cricket. There has been something missing, a lack of connection between the crowd and those in the middle. Maybe that's why I've always enjoyed darts so much. I like its unaffectedness.

There is a danger that cricketers may become so coached (in every way) and so prepared and so on message that the game loses its appeal. It's boring to hear the same interview every time, just as it's boring to watch the same technique all day. If we coach players to become automatons, don't expect people to pay to watch them. I think that's one reason why the Kevin Pietersen story gathered so much momentum. By getting it wrong every now and again, Kevin made himself seem more human. If you over-manage players, all that happens is the public cry out for someone to do something wrong.

This is where Darren Lehmann was a breath of fresh

air for Australian cricket. He is a natural, authentic person. The Aussie public got behind him because they identified with him. The team has bought into that, and played cricket with authenticity. The Big Bash – which everyone can watch – has whipped up public interest about the game; it's buzzing again. The players act as though they are unburdened. Instead of pre-prepared answers, they give the impression of saying what they think. If you're honest, you can't get into trouble. Don't speak in riddles.

In England, for a while we got stuck with clichés and soundbites fed to players before they gave an interview. That's why they endlessly talked about 'some positives we can take out of this'. That really annoys me. If you've had a stinker, just say, 'We were rubbish.' Don't go on about positives. So what if it was a bad performance or you played a bad shot – we've all done it. I have more respect when players say that. Hold up your hand.

Things are improving. This summer's cricket – from the first Test at Lord's against New Zealand to the T20 win against Australia – showed what this new England side is capable of. There's much more to come.

# 14

# THE WHITE ELEPHANT

WHEN people called me 'amateur', they meant it as a term of abuse. But I'd say, 'Thanks very much.' Or if they called me a 'village cricketer', it was supposed to be a hurtful slur. And I'd think, 'Cheers, mate. If it looks like I'm enjoying this, something must be going right.'

Imagine being a professional all the time. It would be rubbish. It would be so boring. After all, what do professionals do? They do things for money. When I played purely as a 'professional' – in the Stanford game, in the IPL – I didn't enjoy it *and* I wasn't very good. Those two facts are connected.

There is a good line about this: the Ark was built by amateurs, the *Titanic* was built by professionals.

In many respects English cricket has become *too* professional. It's obsessed with the system, to the detriment of the game. I worry about young England prospects now getting caught in the 'professional' system, having it drummed into their heads: 'This is how we play cricket, this is how we train, this is how we behave.'

That's very dangerous. I'd much rather they played club cricket on a Saturday afternoon. Go and play county cricket, experience a different social mix. Be natural. Play with authenticity. Have a go. Enjoy everything about the game. That'd be my advice.

One thing you need at the top – and I know because I didn't always have it – is a sense of perspective about what you're doing. Players put too much significance on what they're doing. You can also get lost in your own press sometimes. Taking yourself too seriously is more dangerous than missing practice or being unfit.

Over-professionalism leads to over-complication. Just bowl. Just bat. You're not saving the world. You can never play completely without fear. But you can travel in that direction. Don't put too much pressure on yourself. In the good teams I played in, we allowed ourselves to play.

So what would I do if I was in charge of English cricket? No, don't laugh. But I can't help asking myself what I'd do if I had a blank canvas (apart from bringing back proper woollen cable-knit jumpers).

There are some major structural changes that ought to happen. The worst thing is that the current county system works against good young county players. That's because the England set-up doesn't trust county cricket, so they end up hauling young players into the England system – the endless drudgery of weeks at Loughborough – so they can 'Englandise' them before giving them a go in the team. If the system was fixed, then there would be no need for such a meddling England set-up. You'd just trust the form and performance of county players and pick them, feeling pretty confident that they'd do well.

I remember Duncan Fletcher used to talk openly about 'knocking the "county" out of players', as though county cricket was a disease that only the England management could cure. That's totally wrong. I support county cricket. Personally, I found it harder in many ways than Test cricket. Always playing against different opposition, not getting as used to the bowlers, ropey practice facilities, little time to prepare or practise. No wonder guys like Trescothick, Vaughan and Strauss took to Test cricket straight away. County cricket can be really difficult.

But it is vitally important that the England selectors can trust the county system, so they can pick in-form players without worrying about whether the county opposition was up to scratch. The truth is that in 2015, when the ECB has to provide so much funding for county cricket, it is hard to think of a rational argument for continuing with eighteen counties.

There are simply too many. Almost everyone – I mean everyone in professional cricket: players, coaches, administrators – knows this. But nothing ever changes. Evidence of the problem? How's this. The England team's medical staff monitor fifty-five players in total. Those fifty-five guys, most of whom are in county cricket, are all on England's radar. The England selectors know if any of them gets a niggle, or gains weight, or whatever. It's unlikely that anyone from outside that fifty-five will get picked for the Test team anytime soon. Here's the crucial fact about that group: fifty-two of those fifty-five players come from just twelve counties. So the other six counties contribute only three.

You have to start asking tough questions about those six counties. What are they for? What's their purpose? They obviously can't stand on their own two feet financially. So what exactly are they contributing to English cricket if they aren't providing England players?

Secondly, we should get back to a single, united County Championship – just one division, not two. Then every county would have a chance of winning the premier competition. But for the one-division County Championship to work, there would definitely need to be fewer teams.

Thirdly, we should go back to basics, to the important traditions. Test matches in England should be hosted in the proper venues. The proper venues being Lord's, The Oval, Old Trafford, Headingley, Trent Bridge and Edgbaston. They are the Test match grounds. Everyone else: deal with it. Those are the grounds where players want to play Test matches. I've got no problem with ODIs at Durham and Cardiff and so on. But Test matches should be played at the Test grounds.

My blueprint would blend old traditions with some new departures. We need a new franchise-based Twenty20 league, centred on major cities. England invented T20. Yet we've allowed the rest of the world to move ahead while we've stuck with an eighteen-team tournament.

This new competition has to be available for everyone to watch, free of charge. I understand how much money Sky TV gives to English cricket. But it is vital that at least some cricket is shown on terrestrial TV. The difference between the numbers who watched the 2005 Ashes (on Channel 4) and the 2009 and 2013 Ashes (on Sky) is frightening. There's a generation of England players that most people have never seen play. I now realise how lucky I am that my career overlapped with the old days of terrestrial broadcasting. So I would negotiate with Sky to make sure that the new T20 league was on ITV 4 or something similar.

Next I would get rid of the white elephant at Loughborough that we call the 'National Academy'. Towards the end of my career, I had two full-time jobs. One, England all-rounder. Two, avoiding being sent to Loughborough. I was injured a lot and the England management's solution was always to try to pack me off to Loughborough. But if I'd gone along with that, my career would have been over in 2006.

I was a Lancashire cricketer and, naturally enough, I lived near Lancashire. That's where I bought my house, that's where I wanted to live my life. And I needed to be with Rooster Roberts, who I'd trained with for years. He was much more than a physio to me. He knew how I ticked, knew how to motivate me. He guided me back from injury so many times that I trusted him entirely. It wasn't just a player–physio thing; it was a real partnership.

So why would I want to go to Loughborough for weeks, to live like a student, when I was an established England player with a wife and kids? The Academy was set up to serve England cricket. Instead, Loughborough has become the tail that wags the dog.

The concept of a cricket academy was pioneered in Australia. The idea was to get talented young lads, mostly in their late teens, to learn their cricket in a tough but creative environment. I guess it was part boot camp, part cricket school.

Somehow the English version became totally different. They call it 'mission creep' in the army, when you're supposed to do one thing and end up trying to do far too much. Consider my stints at the Academy and their timing. I'd already played for England before I 'graduated' from the Academy. There's an honours board at Loughborough. And I'm on that. But I'm not really a product of the Academy; I went there as an afterthought. I'm a product of Lancashire cricket. Over the years, the Academy has arranged for almost every promising player to pass through its doors. But that doesn't mean the Academy made them.

The Academy costs English cricket several million pounds a year, yet we don't even own it. The building is rented from the university. The roof in the 'purpose-built' gym is so low you can't do shoulder presses without banging your head. You're expected to sleep in a single bed in a small room with three or four other players.

That's fine for young lads. But I was a grown man with three kids. I'm not going to live in a student bedsit while my wife and kids are at home an hour and a half away. It's pretty simple really. I only share a room with my wife. I don't want to be the width of a bedside table away from someone I don't know.

Much earlier, during one off-season in my early twenties when I was still learning the game, I asked England if I could spend some time at the Academy – I didn't really want to, but I thought I 'ought' to. They said sure, so it was all sorted. And then I was hauled in for a meeting and I was presented with a contract. It was utterly bizarre. It was a three-month contract for £20,000. I couldn't help myself from asking, 'But it says here I'm getting £20,000?' 'What's wrong with that? Is that all right?' came the reply. I was like: 'What? Is that all right? I didn't think I was getting *paid*. I *asked* to come here. Of course it's all right.'

Being at the Academy was like being inside George Orwell's *1984*. Every day you had to be at the gym at 6.30 in the morning. But why? There's twenty-four hours in a day. I can't bat and bowl and train for all of them. I can only train for at most an hour and a half. The result was you'd train at 6.30, then spend the rest of the day wandering around aimlessly. If I'd wanted to be a student,

I'd have gone to university. The only solution for most of us was to go drinking in the student union, just to get through it.

The Academy is a bit like one of those fancy girls' finishing schools. Soon they'll have players balancing books on their heads. But the real problem is that everyone comes out the same and it's damaging the game. I'd knock it down and turn it into affordable housing for students.

Above all, I don't like the arrogance of the place. At Lancashire, I'd be practising with people who'd helped me get to the point of playing for England and doing all right with England. Then they were supposed to be phased out and I was supposed to work with somebody else at Loughborough who didn't know my game at all – but why?

If, that is, you could ever find anyone at Loughborough. Usually, they were too busy doing the 'Level Four' coaching qualification. Level Four is the secret code within English cricket. I'm not saying Level Four is all bad; it can't be. But it's just far too prescriptive, too much by the book – everyone ends up speaking the same, coaching clones.

The latest thing is 'profiling'. They get you to walk around chairs, then tell you if you move from your top half or your bottom half. What type are you? Who gives a toss? I don't care. I just want to hit the ball.

Instead of a coach having an impromptu chat with you, they say, 'How does it feel for you?' as though going on a course teaches you everything about how to connect with people.

It's hard to exaggerate how far this is removed from the original Australian-style Academy. As one of the first intake of English 'academicians', I was sent off there in 2001, to work with Rod Marsh in Adelaide. I don't think it helped me as a player technically, not at all. But I did learn some things about life from chatting with Rod, because he's a tough bastard and mischievous with it. I probably didn't realise at the time how much I was taking in.

Rod got former players to come and talk unguardedly with us. I loved listening to Ian and Greg Chappell when they visited. One minute they'd talk about modern professional stuff. In the next breath they'd talk about Doug Walters, who, legend has it, was drunk every day (he didn't believe in dehydration, so he kept drinking whisky) and used to cough up black tar before he batted.

I'm certainly not advocating that kind of lifestyle now. But when I think of the way cricket has changed, there is a balance to be found between the old war stories and the fussy silliness of ultra-professionalism today. The right place is somewhere in the middle, tending towards the professional side. There always has to be a human element. That's where English cricket is going wrong. And that's why Australia has got it right now with Lehmann as coach.

Central contracts have also gone too far. The idea of central contracts was to take England players out of county cricket, to protect them from being over-bowled by their counties. As a second benefit, central contracts were intended to build the sense of England as a unit, a team rather than just a squad assembled for the match.

I don't want to be a hypocrite, so I should say up front that I was pleased to be given a central contract as a player. I started off with an incremental contract – England tacked a bit extra on your county wages – and then from 2002 I was paid fully by England. What you need is a balance between stability and complacency, between being looked after and becoming too comfortable. There is a danger that getting an England contract leads a player to feel too secure.

So I'd go back to county wages as the basic system and then the prospect of big match fees if you get selected to play for England. No one should be 'secure' in the England side. Everyone should have to fight for it.

While it's important that England players get looked after, it's equally important that they should have proper roots in county cricket, with a club contract. It would also be a good message to current England players: lads, sometimes you need to go back to your clubs and play some good cricket.

The whole of the English game – counties as well as the national team – should be more down to earth, less precious. You hear players turn up at the ground and whinge that the swimming pool in the dressing room is broken, so they can't do their prehab or their rehab or whatever fitness jargon is currently in fashion. Wind your necks in! Go and score some runs and take some wickets. Then we'll worry about the swimming pool in the dressing room.

The culture of endless meetings and dozens of backroom staff has gone way too far. And there are so many people in the tour team photo now that even an ultra-wide-angle lens can't get everyone into the frame.

Off the field, English cricket needed to break down the barriers between ex-players in the media and the current team. It was a real shame, hurting our game. Thankfully, it is now improving.

One story about players and pundits sticks in my mind from my time playing in the Australian Big Bash. There are some real greats up in the commentary box – Ricky Ponting, Mark Waugh, Adam Gilchrist. Anyway, one of my team-mates at Brisbane Heat was a lad called Jimmy Peirson, the Queensland wicketkeeper. He was always talking about Adam Gilchrist, how much he looked up to him. It was non-stop – Gilchrist, Gilchrist, Gilchrist.

So I said to Adam one day, 'Do us a favour, have a chat with Jimmy.' Adam just went straight over and started talking to him about wicketkeeping, trying to help. Next time I saw Jimmy, he couldn't believe it, he was over the moon. Looking at him, you could see just how much a short chat with Adam Gilchrist meant to him.

That sort of thing happens all the time in Australia. When you go to a Test match, you see guys like Mark Taylor and Ian Healy going up to all the players, everyone having a relaxed chat in the middle. All they want is for the team to do well, so they're happy to pass on what they know.

More of that could happen with English cricket. Of course ex-players have got a job to do if they're in the media. And sometimes they have to be critical. But the ex-players should reach out. That goes for helping younger players, too. Who would you rather listen to as an aspiring cricketer: Ian Botham or someone with all the badges? Mike Atherton or an Academy chap? Maybe you won't agree with them, maybe they wouldn't get the message across in the perfect way. But you'd get something out of that forty-five minutes, no question.

It was a positive move to encourage former players to come into the dressing room during 2015. It's the biggest compliment you can get as an ex-player, to be invited back into the rooms. At Chester-le-Street, I took my kids into the dressing room. Then Stuart Broad organised tickets for me at the Lord's Test. That was really nice for me. I sent a little good-luck message to the team before the Ashes and apparently it was well received.

It can only be a good thing if everyone is on board, feeling connected with the England team.

Finally, England's ODI team. For a long time, we've needed to develop an identity as an ODI side. We've never really had that. It is always tempting to copy other teams. If Australia are smashing it with Finch, Warner and Maxwell, the knee-jerk reaction is that England have got to copy them. When India had mystery spinners, we were told to discover a 'doosra' genius. New Zealand have finally found some fast bowlers and so the pundits write that England have to go out and find some quick bowlers. It doesn't work like that, unfortunately. You can't say, 'I know. Let's go down Oxford Street today and pick up some really tall lads and turn them into world-beating quick bowlers.'

We've never actually looked at our ODI cricket and thought, 'You know what, this is what we've got, these are our strengths, we're going to play according to them. We're not going to worry about everyone else. Let's form a one-day identity. This is how we're going to play and we're going to stick to it.'

After the World Cup, it got so bad that my mischievous side wondered whether a nice little sabbatical might not be the best idea. Swap with Ireland for a World Cup; sit it out and play the Associate nations for four years while we figure out a new way of playing!

But the ODIs at the start of the 2015 summer were a refreshing change. We not only played with freedom and flair, we also seemed to be doing it in our own way. We need to stay on that path, developing a pattern and style to our play that fits the players we've got.

\* \* \*

What about the dressing room? If I could say just two things, the central and most basic things, to the present or future England team – sorry, 'group', it's not a team any more, it's a 'group' – they'd be these.

First, you need a sense of perspective on what you're doing – and I didn't always have it. The reason you started playing cricket when you were young is because you liked it, because you enjoyed playing it. And I'm not saying you don't enjoy it now. But it's easy to pile too much on top. You're only bowling and batting, you know. Go out there and have fun. You'll never play completely without fear (much as it would be lovely). But don't put all the pressure on yourself, don't map out every scenario. When you bat, go and hit it. Go out and enjoy it. Just bowl. It isn't that important, honestly it isn't. It isn't a war zone in Africa. You're only trying to hit a few wickets.

Secondly, naturalness is priceless in sport. I look back on my career and realise that the most robust parts of my game were the least coached. And the times when my game became really vulnerable were when I got too worried about technique. Things you learn for yourself stay learnt. Things that were grafted on by someone else can fall apart.

After 2005, I made the mistake of taking batting too seriously. I took on too much information, like that silly forward press and the trigger movements that Duncan was always going on about. I still can't tell you what a trigger movement is. I started moving around in the crease and doing this, that and the other. It threw me off.

But my bowling was the opposite. Because I regarded myself as primarily a batter, I never really worried about bowling. In retrospect, I can see how that created valuable space for my bowling to develop naturally and intuitively. My bowling was never over-coached and that was its biggest strength. It held together under pressure.

There were just two simple things on my bowling checklist. One, to get my left arm up high; two, to follow through well. My bowling broke just about every rule in the coaching book. But every player needs to find his own way, a style that fits his own body and temperament.

When I ran in and bowled, I'd think, 'Oh, this is graceful, look at this, wow.' I'd have this picture in my head of myself in full flight, moving smoothly and then jumping at the crease. 'Oh, it's nice that,' I'd tell myself, 'following through really nicely. Oh, that's good. Michael Holding, eat your heart out. Look at this!'

One day, I saw it back on a TV replay. Oh, my word. Horrible. In the run-up, it looked like my shoelaces were tied together. By the time I eventually got to the bowling crease, I fell away, and it seemed to require a huge effort to hurl the arm over, a tangle of limbs.

Textbook? Far from it. But I was lucky it was never trained out of me. And I'm now inclined to give Troy Cooley, who was England's bowling coach in 2005, more credit than I did back then for not messing around with my action. I hope that future generations of England players will be able to say the same thing. When I have the occasional net with young pros now, I might bat against several different bowlers and yet it seems like I've only faced one. They're all the same, schooled in the 'straight lines' biomechanics that's so fashionable. Yet it's obviously a weakness if a bowling attack lacks variety.

Last winter, I popped in to see the England team when they were in Brisbane. I saw Steven Finn bowling on his own, in the nets, just the stumps to aim at. I went over and said, 'What are you doing? Are you working on something?' He said, 'Oh, my arms get short when I bowl.' I said, 'Stick your arms out, let's have a look at them.' They weren't short, they looked massive!

So I just said, 'Do you like bowling?' He said, 'Yeah.' I said, 'Do you like bowling fast?' 'Yeah.' I said, 'So just run up, jump, bowl it fast. None of this thinking about crossing your legs over or your arms getting short. Run in, bowl fast, somewhere down that end.'

Look at Steve Smith's batting technique. He's been ranked as the best batsman in the world. Technically, I just don't get him. His feet are stuck together. He wobbles across his crease. He looks awful. And he gets loads of runs. Why? Because he just plays, rather than fretting about appearances.

# 15

# PAST AND PRESENT

PRESTON still feels like home. When I go to Preston, drive through it or just see the road sign, I feel a sense of belonging. I grew up in Preston, my parents still live in Preston and I love going back there. When people ask where I'm from, I usually say Preston.

I don't live in Preston now, though we have moved back nearby. And I feel really settled – the familiarity, the routine, the people I see. Living close to 'home' without being located exactly where I grew up seems about right. The geography echoes how I feel. In life, I'm gradually rejoining my old world, the places and people who shaped me. We've travelled a lot, lived in such different places, and yet we've ended up not a million miles away from where we started. I like that.

But I also accept that I'm a different man now. You can pretend you're exactly the same working-class kid, but it's not true. I'll never entirely fit in anywhere.

We lived in Dubai, then we moved to Surrey. I've no regrets about the spells I had living in other places. I don't mind something going wrong. I don't want to look back when I'm sixty and think, 'Oh, we had a chance to do this, but we never did it.' But I carried around my own baggage with me. You can move all you like – you'll have the same issues. I could be sat in a shoe box with my kids, or I could be the king of England, it doesn't matter: I'd still have all my baggage with me. Only in the past two years have I looked at myself and realised what I do and don't need.

The spell in Dubai was important because I had to get away from cricket. I'd retired and there was a grieving process. I thought: new start, fresh beginnings. The problem was that I was still hankering to play. I couldn't get over that. It's wrong to try to fill that void straight away. I could have lived in Buckingham Palace at that time and I'd have hated it there, too. The problem wasn't Dubai, it was me.

Next we moved to Cobham. Surrey definitely wasn't my cup of tea. After a while I looked round and realised I didn't have anything in common with the people I was knocking around with. Didn't relate to them. The things they were talking about – how big their house was, the holiday home in Chamonix, the latest handbag the wife had bought – I'm really not bothered.

Instead of getting to know them as people, I got to know what they aspired to, what they wanted. All I could see was image and front and one-upmanship – who's got more, who's got the most. Some of the dinner parties we went to in Cobham were desperate. It was more competitive than the Ashes.

To amuse myself, I started making things up. One guest would brag about having just been heliskiing through inches of perfect powder snow, so I'd come up with something ridiculous. Just lies, to see how far I could push the absurdity of it all. They would carry on competing with me even though I was making it all up.

Alternatively, I would lose interest completely, which is a problem for me as I'm not always entirely in control of my facial expression, so I give away what I'm feeling. That's when the missus kicks me under the table and says, 'Look interested!' Worst-case scenario is when I slip into dressing-room mode and start really taking the mickey. Things that might sound acceptable in the dressing room don't always go down so well at an aspirational dining table in Cobham. Yeah, better just to leave and go home.

At one point, probably in my mid-twenties, I was closer to that world – wanting the fast car, the big house, money in the bank. Early on, there were times when, even though I had the cars and the house, I couldn't actually afford any of it. I was spending more than I was bringing in. There's no real future in that. Then I earned more and more, until eventually I thought, 'What's the point?'

Now? We're selling our house to get a smaller one; I drive a practical hybrid car. These things don't interest me any more. I've tired of looking into the future, imagining all the things I want to have. As long as I've got enough money to pay my mortgage and put the kids through school and have a nice life, what is the rest for? It's just nonsense. I've had friends who've had loads of money and no happiness.

I've also seen material competitiveness destroy relationships in dressing rooms. People end up worrying about what someone else is earning and whether they're missing out. I see it now with cricketers in retirement. They're so preoccupied by what everyone else is doing that they can't be happy for themselves. Success isn't about things we acquire.

I'm gradually getting rid of all the things I don't need. I've only been to the end of my garden about eight times. Why do I need so much? We've got a big house but we basically live in the kitchen. The pool table? I've probably played about six frames.

It's what I always thought I wanted. But it isn't. We get embarrassed when people come round. My Preston mates haven't been to my house. How can I show that house to a man who works twelve hours a day? Last winter we had a great time in Australia living in a three-bedroom flat as a family. We loved it.

I'm a little bit jealous of my old friends who work hard, live a normal life and know where they stand. But much as I respect that life and feel a pang of envy, I also know I couldn't have done it myself. No chance. There was an innate desire to do new things, push myself, find my limits, keep moving. That is bound up with worldly things, too, and you end up in a different place from where you started.

I've got a foot in both camps. One day I'll be at Nando's in Preston, half-price on a Monday lunch; the next I'll be eating sushi at Zuma in Knightsbridge. I like travelling in the front of the plane. And I still want to be working class. But I'm not.

Much as I feel more comfortable around my old mates, there are differences. For example, it's probably in my interests to vote Tory. I did once and made the mistake of telling my dad – he didn't speak to me for ages. You feel like you're cheating on your family.

I'm not good at keeping in touch, even with close friends. I don't mind just picking up where we left off, even after a break of a few years. I dislike the whole process of going through what I've been up to. It embarrasses me. Above all, I'm not a particularly needy person. I'm not twelve. But I should understand that some people are needy. Maybe that's why I'm not always good at relationships. But I think I'm gradually recalibrating myself, finding a balance between the different sides of my character. Part of that is just reconnecting with people.

I lost interest in the whole material game when I lost a lot of money. It's not crippled us and we're not struggling. If I was really money-driven, I think that would keep me awake at night, festering away at the back of my mind. But it doesn't. It is what it is.

And I learnt I'd put too much trust in other people. When you play professional sport you put your trust in financial advisers and hangers-on who you think have your best interests at heart. They come to christenings and family gatherings; it's as though they're your mates. And then you finish your career and you try and get a grip of everything, to see what's left. And they've promised you the world and given you an atlas.

It was like . . . bloody hell, what have we ended up with here? Bills coming out of my ears for stuff that they put us into. Losing a lot of the money I'd earned. Nonexistent contracts for some of the work I did. And some of the people who made the decisions – they just went missing.

I wouldn't expect or seek any sympathy – I made some good money and lost some, too. And I should have taken more responsibility. You develop a dependency on people. That's not wise; it's just wrong.

The experience has made me a lot more guarded, which is not my natural character. There's a voice in my head now that says, 'Just check this out, make sure this is fine.'

Cricket? When I walked off the field at The Oval in 2009, the first question put to me on the Sky coverage was 'Do you think you're a great player?' What? I couldn't believe it. What a question. I never set out to be a 'great player'. Great player, not a great player. Couldn't care less. I had a go. I enjoyed it. That's what I wanted to do.

In my book there are maybe a handful of great players in the history of the game. Me? I was all right. People say my statistics don't stack up to the recognition I get. I'd agree with that. But I wouldn't swap my career with anyone else's.

I'm more interested in how I fronted up against top sides than in averages and aggregates. I did all right in the big games. In the era in which I played cricket, the best team in the world was Australia. I played against them in three Test series – did well, did badly, did OK third time around. The second-best team was South Africa. I played pretty well against them.

Now I've got a little bit older I've become a cricket fan again. I take my two sons to games, sitting in the crowd. I actually really like it. I accept that cricket will always be there in my life, but *playing* cricket isn't the future. Took me a while to understand that.

I've also learnt that cricket gave me things I still need, even though I resisted them at the time. As a cricketer, you have an automatic sense of belonging, you know where you are, you know what you're doing. Yet I always resisted the patterns and routines of professional sport. I wore the wrong clothes, turned up late, pushed the boundaries, sometimes just for the sake of it. Now I can see that I need some of that sense of routine and pattern. Otherwise you just drift.

But I don't miss the defence mechanism I built up to deal with my struggles in cricket. The performer is still inside me, but I don't need the persona. I've laid my cards on the table. I don't have to pretend to anyone any more.

It is a lot easier to be authentic when you know you've been honest.

It sounds perverse, but I feel even my mistakes had some useful purpose. I just wish I'd learnt from them more quickly.

The future? I'd like to have something I can grow and nurture, something that's mine, perhaps my own TV or radio show, that I can improve and get better at – a reason to get up each day and work hard.

In one respect, TV presenting is very different to sport. Sport is objective and quantifiable. You know where you stand: take runs and score wickets and you play in the next match. You're in control. I didn't need to be told if I played well. I didn't need to be told I'd been selected. You knew when you'd done enough. In TV, the decisions are all subjective. You could have the best idea and someone behind a desk might say no. I'm not naturally patient. I'm especially impatient when dealing with subjective criteria.

For all my adventures after cricket, there are moments when ordinary life looks very attractive. I take the kids to school sometimes and I look at all the dads in their suits and ties, and I think, 'You've got a job, haven't you? You're doing something today. You'll have a sense of purpose and belonging.' Me, I'll go to the gym, have a coffee with the OAPs afterwards and then I'll probably watch a bit of *Storage Wars* on TV before picking up the kids. From my perspective, there's a lot to be said for the rhythm of ordinary life.

It used to annoy me inside professional cricket when players would have a go at a player for being 'content'. Just because someone was enjoying his level, not striving for perfection or greatness, not trying to be the best in the world, they'd slag him off: 'He's happy. He's in a comfort zone.'

Well, I wish I'd been like that: turn up, play, go home, feel happy. Would you prefer that or what I felt? Always striving to be better, for perfection, never satisfied. Whatever I did, it was never good enough. I was always trying to do something better straight away.

But I can also see that *not* being content has put me into so many interesting situations in my life.

Maybe the grass always looks greener on the other side. I'm not sure I would ever have been happy settling down to a completely routine life. I'd always find a cliff edge to walk along soon enough.

Whatever I do have, I'll always imagine what it's like to have the opposite.

Fred, Andrew, Fred, Andrew.

# ACKNOWLEDGEMENTS

I HAVE written about highlights from my career in other books, but this is the first totally forthright account of the whole story.

The book grew out of a series of honest and enjoyable conversations with Ed Smith. He grasped what I wanted to say and helped me to say it. I was glad to resume a partnership with a former team-mate.

I'm grateful to Hodder & Stoughton, my long-standing publisher. Roddy Bloomfield and his team of Tim Waller, Fiona Rose and Veronique Norton were patient and supportive throughout.

Thanks also to my agents Richard Thompson for his valued guidance and Kate Lydon for her brutally honest feedback!

Finally, much of this story would have been impossible without the love and support of my family – my wife Rachael and children Holly, Rocky and Corey. I owe just about everything to them.

# PICTURE
# ACKNOWLEDGEMENTS

The author and publisher would like to thank the following for permission to reproduce photographs:

Daniel Bowring, Philip Brown, Winston Bynorth, Camera Press London, Gareth Copley/PA Archive/PA Images/Getty Images, Graham Chadwick/ Rex Shutterstock, cricketpix. com, Daily Mail/Rex Shutterstock, Adam Davy/Empics Sport/PA Images, Discovery Communications, Kieran Doherty/Reuters, Justin Downing/REX Shutterstock, Stu Forster/Getty Images, Gareth Fuller/PA Archive/PA Images, Fullwell73, James Gourley/REX Shutterstock, Richard Heathcote/Getty Images, Scott Heavey/Getty Images, Jonathan Hordle/Rex Shutterstock, Chris Hyde/ Cricket Australia/Getty Images, ITV/ Rex Shutterstock, ©Tom Jenkins/The Guardian, Lancashire Evening Post, Dylan Martinez/Reuters/Action Images, Graham Morris/

Cricketpix, Warren Orchard/ BBC, Clive Rose/ Getty Images, Roving Enterprises, Tom Shaw/Getty Images, Sky UK, Craig Sugden, Justin Tallis/Getty Images, Dave Thompson/Press Association Images, tvf Media

All other photographs are from private collections.

# TEST CAREER STATISTICS

*Compiled by Benedict Bermange*

| OVERALL RECORD | M | Inns | NO | Runs | HS | Avge | SR | 100 | 50 | Ct | Balls | Runs | Wkts | Avge | BB | 5I |
|---|---|---|---|---|---|---|---|---|---|---|---|---|---|---|---|---|
| Test matches | 79 | 130 | 9 | 3845 | 167 | 31.77 | 62.05 | 5 | 26 | 52 | 14951 | 7410 | 226 | 32.78 | 5-58 | 3 |

| BY OPPONENT | M | Inns | NO | Runs | HS | Avge | SR | 100 | 50 | Ct | Balls | Runs | Wkts | Avge | BB | 5I |
|---|---|---|---|---|---|---|---|---|---|---|---|---|---|---|---|---|
| Australia | 15 | 29 | 2 | 906 | 102 | 33.55 | 67.76 | 1 | 6 | 4 | 2963 | 1660 | 50 | 33.20 | 5-78 | 2 |
| Bangladesh | 2 | | | | | | | | | 1 | 221 | 138 | 9 | 15.33 | 3-44 | 0 |
| India | 11 | 18 | 0 | 473 | 70 | 26.27 | 51.35 | 0 | 6 | 9 | 2358 | 1088 | 29 | 37.51 | 4-50 | 0 |
| New Zealand | 6 | 10 | 0 | 459 | 137 | 45.90 | 79.13 | 1 | 4 | 4 | 1187 | 604 | 19 | 31.78 | 3-49 | 0 |
| Pakistan | 3 | 6 | 0 | 125 | 56 | 20.83 | 54.82 | 0 | 1 | 3 | 841 | 409 | 13 | 31.46 | 4-68 | 0 |
| South Africa | 19 | 32 | 3 | 935 | 142 | 32.24 | 62.20 | 1 | 5 | 8 | 3649 | 1796 | 48 | 37.41 | 4-44 | 0 |
| Sri Lanka | 9 | 14 | 2 | 232 | 77 | 19.33 | 53.70 | 0 | 1 | 8 | 1997 | 887 | 27 | 32.85 | 3-42 | 0 |
| West Indies | 12 | 18 | 2 | 682 | 167 | 42.62 | 63.44 | 2 | 3 | 15 | 1657 | 793 | 31 | 25.58 | 5-58 | 1 |
| Zimbabwe | 2 | 3 | 0 | 33 | 16 | 11.00 | 27.50 | 0 | 0 | 0 | 78 | 35 | 0 | - | - | 0 |

| BY COUNTRY | M | Inns | NO | Runs | HS | Avge | SR | 100 | 50 | Ct | Balls | Runs | Wkts | Avge | BB | 5I |
|---|---|---|---|---|---|---|---|---|---|---|---|---|---|---|---|---|
| Australia | 6 | 12 | 1 | 304 | 89 | 27.63 | 58.46 | 0 | 2 | 0 | 1026 | 588 | 18 | 32.66 | 4-59 | 0 |
| England | 40 | 63 | 6 | 2007 | 167 | 35.21 | 69.93 | 3 | 14 | 28 | 7661 | 3936 | 109 | 36.11 | 5-78 | 2 |
| India | 8 | 13 | 0 | 374 | 70 | 28.76 | 46.86 | 0 | 5 | 6 | 1686 | 731 | 24 | 30.45 | 4-50 | 0 |
| New Zealand | 3 | 6 | 0 | 243 | 137 | 40.50 | 94.55 | 1 | 1 | 2 | 558 | 313 | 9 | 34.77 | 3-49 | 0 |
| Pakistan | 3 | 6 | 0 | 125 | 56 | 20.83 | 54.82 | 0 | 1 | 3 | 841 | 409 | 13 | 31.46 | 4-68 | 0 |
| South Africa | 9 | 15 | 1 | 382 | 77 | 27.28 | 55.28 | 0 | 2 | 4 | 1609 | 764 | 28 | 27.28 | 4-44 | 0 |
| Sri Lanka | 3 | 6 | 0 | 143 | 77 | 23.83 | 53.96 | 0 | 1 | 0 | 582 | 221 | 9 | 24.55 | 3-42 | 0 |
| West Indies | 7 | 9 | 1 | 267 | 102 | 33.37 | 47.08 | 1 | 0 | 9 | 988 | 448 | 16 | 28.00 | 5-58 | 1 |

| BY CONTINENT | M | Inns | NO | Runs | HS | Avge | SR | 100 | 50 | Ct | Balls | Runs | Wkts | Avge | BB | 5I |
|---|---|---|---|---|---|---|---|---|---|---|---|---|---|---|---|---|
| Africa | 9 | 15 | 1 | 382 | 77 | 27.28 | 55.28 | 0 | 2 | 4 | 1609 | 764 | 28 | 27.28 | 4-44 | 0 |
| Americas | 7 | 9 | 1 | 267 | 102 | 33.37 | 47.08 | 1 | 0 | 9 | 988 | 448 | 16 | 28.00 | 5-58 | 1 |
| Asia | 14 | 25 | 0 | 642 | 77 | 25.68 | 49.72 | 0 | 7 | 9 | 3109 | 1361 | 46 | 29.58 | 4-50 | 0 |
| Australasia | 9 | 18 | 1 | 547 | 137 | 32.17 | 70.39 | 1 | 3 | 2 | 1584 | 901 | 27 | 33.37 | 4-59 | 0 |
| Europe | 40 | 63 | 6 | 2007 | 167 | 35.21 | 69.93 | 3 | 14 | 28 | 7661 | 3936 | 109 | 36.11 | 5-78 | 2 |

| HOME AND AWAY | M | Inns | NO | Runs | HS | Avge | SR | 100 | 50 | Ct | Balls | Runs | Wkts | Avge | BB | 5I |
|---|---|---|---|---|---|---|---|---|---|---|---|---|---|---|---|---|
| Home | 40 | 63 | 6 | 2007 | 167 | 35.21 | 69.93 | 3 | 14 | 28 | 7661 | 3936 | 109 | 36.11 | 5-78 | 2 |
| Away | 39 | 67 | 3 | 1838 | 137 | 28.71 | 55.26 | 2 | 12 | 24 | 7290 | 3474 | 117 | 29.69 | 5-58 | 1 |

| BY YEAR | M | Inns | NO | Runs | HS | Avge | SR | 100 | 50 | Ct | Balls | Runs | Wkts | Avge | BB | 5I |
|---|---|---|---|---|---|---|---|---|---|---|---|---|---|---|---|---|
| 1998 | 2 | 3 | 0 | 17 | 17 | 5.66 | 37.77 | 0 | 0 | 1 | 210 | 112 | 1 | 112.00 | 1-52 | 0 |
| 1999 | 3 | 5 | 0 | 133 | 42 | 26.60 | 71.89 | 0 | 0 | 2 | 377 | 174 | 5 | 34.80 | 2-31 | 0 |
| 2000 | 4 | 6 | 0 | 83 | 22 | 13.83 | 39.71 | 0 | 0 | 1 | 240 | 99 | 1 | 99.00 | 1-48 | 0 |
| 2001 | 3 | 5 | 0 | 26 | 18 | 5.20 | 50.98 | 0 | 0 | 1 | 552 | 189 | 6 | 31.50 | 4-50 | 0 |
| 2002 | 9 | 14 | 0 | 384 | 137 | 27.42 | 84.02 | 1 | 2 | 9 | 1872 | 982 | 20 | 49.10 | 3-49 | 0 |
| 2003 | 8 | 14 | 0 | 566 | 142 | 40.42 | 70.75 | 1 | 4 | 0 | 1674 | 813 | 19 | 42.78 | 3-42 | 0 |
| 2004 | 13 | 19 | 2 | 898 | 167 | 52.82 | 66.71 | 2 | 7 | 16 | 2218 | 1108 | 43 | 25.76 | 5-58 | 1 |
| 2005 | 14 | 24 | 1 | 709 | 102 | 30.82 | 64.57 | 1 | 5 | 7 | 3194 | 1660 | 68 | 24.41 | 5-78 | 1 |
| 2006 | 10 | 18 | 3 | 469 | 70 | 31.26 | 51.36 | 0 | 5 | 7 | 2123 | 1115 | 33 | 33.78 | 4-96 | 0 |
| 2007 | 1 | 2 | 0 | 96 | 89 | 48.00 | 58.89 | 0 | 1 | 0 | 102 | 56 | 1 | 56.00 | 1-56 | 0 |
| 2008 | 5 | 9 | 2 | 197 | 62 | 28.14 | 43.77 | 0 | 1 | 5 | 1242 | 534 | 16 | 33.37 | 4-89 | 0 |
| 2009 | 7 | 11 | 1 | 267 | 74 | 26.70 | 55.74 | 0 | 1 | 3 | 1147 | 568 | 13 | 43.69 | 5-92 | 1 |

| BY CAPTAIN | M | Inns | NO | Runs | HS | Avge | SR | 100 | 50 | Ct | Balls | Runs | Wkts | Avge | BB | 5I |
|---|---|---|---|---|---|---|---|---|---|---|---|---|---|---|---|---|
| A Flintoff | 11 | 20 | 3 | 565 | 89 | 33.23 | 52.50 | 0 | 6 | 7 | 2225 | 1171 | 34 | 34.44 | 4-96 | 0 |
| N Hussain | 20 | 31 | 1 | 666 | 137 | 21.48 | 69.44 | 1 | 2 | 13 | 3203 | 1557 | 32 | 48.65 | 4-50 | 0 |
| KP Pietersen | 3 | 5 | 1 | 104 | 62 | 26.00 | 42.44 | 0 | 1 | 3 | 702 | 296 | 9 | 32.88 | 3-49 | 0 |
| GC Smith | 1 | 2 | 0 | 50 | 35 | 25.00 | 79.36 | 0 | 0 | 0 | 204 | 107 | 7 | 15.28 | 4-59 | 0 |
| AJ Stewart | 2 | 3 | 0 | 17 | 17 | 5.66 | 37.77 | 0 | 0 | 1 | 210 | 112 | 1 | 112.00 | 1-52 | 0 |
| AJ Strauss | 7 | 11 | 1 | 267 | 74 | 26.70 | 55.74 | 0 | 1 | 3 | 1147 | 568 | 13 | 43.69 | 5-92 | 1 |
| ME Trescothick | 2 | 3 | 0 | 119 | 63 | 39.66 | 66.85 | 0 | 1 | 0 | 515 | 259 | 11 | 23.54 | 4-68 | 0 |
| MP Vaughan | 33 | 55 | 4 | 2057 | 167 | 40.33 | 65.28 | 4 | 15 | 25 | 6745 | 3340 | 119 | 28.06 | 5-58 | 2 |

| BY RESULT | M | Inns | NO | Runs | HS | Avge | SR | 100 | 50 | Ct | Balls | Runs | Wkts | Avge | BB | 5I |
|---|---|---|---|---|---|---|---|---|---|---|---|---|---|---|---|---|
| Won | 30 | 44 | 4 | 1572 | 167 | 39.30 | 70.87 | 3 | 12 | 28 | 5153 | 2668 | 92 | 29.00 | 5-58 | 2 |
| Lost | 25 | 49 | 2 | 1251 | 142 | 26.61 | 56.58 | 1 | 7 | 11 | 4799 | 2467 | 73 | 33.79 | 4-59 | 0 |
| Drawn | 24 | 37 | 3 | 1022 | 102 | 30.05 | 57.83 | 1 | 7 | 13 | 4999 | 2275 | 61 | 37.29 | 5-78 | 1 |

| TESTS – SERIES BY SERIES | M | Inns | NO | Runs | HS | Avge | SR | 100 | 50 | Ct | Balls | Runs | Wkts | Avge | BB | 5I |
|---|---|---|---|---|---|---|---|---|---|---|---|---|---|---|---|---|
| South Africa in England 1998 | 2 | 3 | 0 | 17 | 17 | 5.66 | 37.77 | 0 | 0 | 1 | 210 | 112 | 1 | 112.00 | 1-52 | 0 |
| England in South Africa 1999–00 | 4 | 6 | 0 | 155 | 42 | 25.83 | 66.81 | 0 | 0 | 2 | 401 | 190 | 5 | 38.00 | 2-31 | 0 |
| Zimbabwe in England 2000 | 2 | 3 | 0 | 33 | 16 | 11.00 | 27.50 | 0 | 0 | 0 | 78 | 35 | 0 | – | – | 0 |
| West Indies in England 2000 | 1 | 2 | 0 | 28 | 16 | 14.00 | 66.66 | 0 | 0 | 1 | 138 | 48 | 1 | 48.00 | 1-48 | 0 |
| England in India 2001–02 | 3 | 5 | 0 | 26 | 18 | 5.20 | 50.98 | 0 | 0 | 1 | 552 | 189 | 6 | 31.50 | 4-50 | 0 |
| England in New Zealand 2001–02 | 3 | 6 | 0 | 243 | 137 | 40.50 | 94.55 | 1 | 1 | 2 | 558 | 313 | 9 | 34.77 | 3-49 | 0 |
| Sri Lanka in England 2002 | 3 | 3 | 0 | 42 | 29 | 14.00 | 54.54 | 0 | 0 | 4 | 642 | 312 | 6 | 52.00 | 2-27 | 0 |
| India in England 2002 | 3 | 5 | 0 | 99 | 59 | 19.80 | 80.48 | 0 | 1 | 3 | 672 | 357 | 5 | 71.40 | 2-22 | 0 |
| South Africa in England 2003 | 5 | 8 | 0 | 423 | 142 | 52.87 | 79.06 | 1 | 3 | 0 | 1092 | 592 | 10 | 59.20 | 2-55 | 0 |
| England in Sri Lanka 2003–04 | 3 | 6 | 0 | 143 | 77 | 23.83 | 53.96 | 0 | 1 | 7 | 582 | 221 | 9 | 24.55 | 3-42 | 0 |
| England in West Indies 2003–04 | 4 | 5 | 1 | 200 | 102* | 50.00 | 55.09 | 1 | 0 | 2 | 614 | 297 | 11 | 27.00 | 5-58 | 1 |
| New Zealand in England 2004 | 3 | 4 | 0 | 216 | 94 | 54.00 | 66.87 | 0 | 3 | 2 | 629 | 291 | 10 | 29.10 | 3-60 | 0 |
| West Indies in England 2004 | 4 | 7 | 1 | 387 | 167 | 64.50 | 83.04 | 1 | 3 | 5 | 531 | 297 | 14 | 21.21 | 3-25 | 0 |
| England in South Africa 2004–05 | 5 | 9 | 1 | 227 | 77 | 28.37 | 49.45 | 0 | 2 | 2 | 1208 | 574 | 23 | 24.95 | 4-44 | 0 |
| Bangladesh in England 2005 | 2 | 1 | – | – | – | – | – | 0 | 0 | 1 | 221 | 138 | 9 | 15.33 | 3-44 | 0 |
| Australia in England 2005 | 5 | 10 | 0 | 402 | 102 | 40.20 | 74.16 | 1 | 3 | 3 | 1164 | 655 | 24 | 27.29 | 5-78 | 1 |
| ICC Super Series 2005–06 | 1 | 2 | 0 | 50 | 35 | 25.00 | 79.36 | 0 | 0 | 0 | 204 | 107 | 7 | 15.28 | 4-59 | 0 |
| England in Pakistan 2005–06 | 3 | 6 | 0 | 125 | 56 | 20.83 | 54.82 | 0 | 1 | 3 | 841 | 409 | 13 | 31.46 | 4-68 | 0 |
| England in India 2005–06 | 3 | 5 | 0 | 264 | 70 | 52.80 | 49.90 | 0 | 4 | 3 | 630 | 336 | 11 | 30.54 | 4-96 | 0 |
| Sri Lanka in England 2006 | 3 | 5 | 2 | 47 | 33* | 15.66 | 52.22 | 0 | 0 | 4 | 773 | 354 | 12 | 29.50 | 3-52 | 0 |
| England in Australia 2006–07 | 5 | 10 | 1 | 254 | 89 | 28.22 | 55.57 | 0 | 2 | 0 | 822 | 481 | 11 | 43.72 | 4-99 | 0 |
| South Africa in England 2008 | 3 | 6 | 2 | 113 | 38 | 28.25 | 48.70 | 0 | 0 | 3 | 738 | 328 | 9 | 36.44 | 4-89 | 0 |
| England in India 2008–09 | 2 | 3 | 0 | 84 | 62 | 28.00 | 38.53 | 0 | 1 | 2 | 504 | 206 | 7 | 29.42 | 3-49 | 0 |
| England in West Indies 2008–09 | 3 | 4 | 0 | 67 | 43 | 16.75 | 32.84 | 0 | 0 | 2 | 374 | 151 | 5 | 30.20 | 3-47 | 0 |
| Australia in England 2009 | 4 | 7 | 1 | 200 | 74 | 33.33 | 72.72 | 0 | 1 | 1 | 773 | 417 | 8 | 52.12 | 5-92 | 1 |

**TESTS – MATCH BY MATCH**

| | Team | Opponent | Venue | Batting | Bowling | Catches |
|---|---|---|---|---|---|---|
| 23/7/1998 | England | South Africa | Nottingham | 17 | 1-52 & 0-16 | |
| 6/8/1998 | England | South Africa | Leeds | 0 & 0 | 0-31 & 0-13 | 1 |
| 25/11/1999 | England | South Africa | Johannesburg | 38 & 36 | 0-45 | |
| 9/12/1999 | England | South Africa | Port Elizabeth | 42 & 12 | 2-31 & 1-24 | 2 |
| 26/12/1999 | England | South Africa | Durban | 5 | 0-7 & 2-67 | |
| 2/1/2000 | England | South Africa | Cape Town | 22 | 0-16 | |
| 18/5/2000 | England | Zimbabwe | Lord's | 1 | 0-2 | |
| 1/6/2000 | England | Zimbabwe | Nottingham | 16 & 16 | 0-33 | |
| 15/6/2000 | England | West Indies | Birmingham | 16 & 12 | 1-48 | 1 |
| 3/12/2001 | England | India | Mohali | 18 & 4 | 0-80 | |
| 11/12/2001 | England | India | Ahmedabad | 0 & 4 | 2-42 & 0-17 | 1 |
| 19/12/2001 | England | India | Bangalore | 0 | 4-50 | |
| 13/3/2002 | England | New Zealand | Chr:stchurch | 0 & 137 | 0-29 & 2-94 | 2 |
| 21/3/2002 | England | New Zealand | Wellington | 2 & 75 | 0-9 & 1-24 | |
| 30/3/2002 | England | New Zealand | Auckland | 29 & 0 | 3-49 & 3-108 | |
| 16/5/2002 | England | Sri Lanka | Lord's | 12 | 2-101 & 0-18 | 1 |
| 30/5/2002 | England | Sri Lanka | Birmingham | 29 | 2-27 & 0-23 | 2 |
| 13/6/2002 | England | Sri Lanka | Manchester | 1 | 1-65 & 1-78 | 1 |
| 25/7/2002 | England | India | Lord's | 59 & 7 | 2-22 & 0-87 | 1 |
| 8/8/2002 | England | India | Nottingham | 33 | 1-85 & 1-95 | 1 |
| 22/8/2002 | England | India | Leeds | 0 & 0 | 1-68 | 1 |
| 24/7/2003 | England | South Africa | Birmingham | 40 | 0-97 & 0-16 | |
| 31/7/2003 | England | South Africa | Lord's | 11 & 142 | 1-115 | |

**TESTS – MATCH BY MATCH** *(continued)*

| | Team | Opponent | Venue | Batting | Bowling | Catches |
|---|---|---|---|---|---|---|
| 14/8/2003 | England | South Africa | Nottingham | 0 & 30 | 2-91 & 1-54 | |
| 21/8/2003 | England | South Africa | Leeds | 55 & 50 | 2-55 & 2-63 | 3 |
| 4/9/2003 | England | South Africa | The Oval | 95 | 1-88 & 1-13 | 2 |
| 2/12/2003 | England | Sri Lanka | Galle | 1 & 0 | 3-42 & 1-32 | 2 |
| 10/12/2003 | England | Sri Lanka | Kandy | 16 & 19 | 2-60 & 1-40 | |
| 18/12/2003 | England | Sri Lanka | Colombo–SSC | 77 & 30 | 2-47 | |
| 11/3/2004 | England | West Indies | Kingston | 46 | 1-45 | 3 |
| 19/3/2004 | England | West Indies | Port-of-Spain | 23 | 0-38 & 2-27 | 2 |
| 1/4/2004 | England | West Indies | Bridgetown | 15 | 5-58 & 2-20 | 2 |
| 10/4/2004 | England | West Indies | St John's | 102* & 14 | 1-109 | |
| 20/5/2004 | England | New Zealand | Lord's | 63 | 2-63 & 1-40 | |
| 3/6/2004 | England | New Zealand | Leeds | 94 | 2-64 & 1-16 | 2 |
| 10/6/2004 | England | New Zealand | Nottingham | 54 & 5 | 1-48 & 3-60 | |
| 22/7/2004 | England | West Indies | Lord's | 6 & 58 | 3-25 & 1-0 | |
| 29/7/2004 | England | West Indies | Birmingham | 167 & 20 | 2-52 & 0-19 | 2 |
| 12/8/2004 | England | West Indies | Manchester | 7 & 57* | 3-79 & 3-26 | 2 |
| 19/8/2004 | England | West Indies | The Oval | 72 | 1-32 & 1-64 | 1 |
| 17/12/2004 | England | South Africa | Port Elizabeth | 35 | 3-72 & 2-47 | 1 |
| 26/12/2004 | England | South Africa | Durban | 0 & 60 | 2-66 & 1-38 | 1 |
| 2/1/2005 | England | South Africa | Cape Town | 12 & 20 | 4-79 & 2-46 | |
| 13/1/2005 | England | South Africa | Johannesburg | 2 & 7 | 1-77 & 2-59 | |
| 21/1/2005 | England | South Africa | Centurion | 77 & 14* | 4-44 & 2-46 | |
| 26/5/2005 | England | Bangladesh | Lord's | DNB | 2-22 & 3-44 | 1 |
| 3/6/2005 | England | Bangladesh | Chester-le-Street | DNB | 1-14 & 3-58 | |
| 21/7/2005 | England | Australia | Lord's | 0 & 3 | 2-50 & 2-123 | |
| 4/8/2005 | England | Australia | Birmingham | 68 & 73 | 3-52 & 4-79 | 2 |

| Date | Team | Opposition | Venue | Batting | Bowling | |
|---|---|---|---|---|---|---|
| 18/ / | England | Australia | Nottingham | 102 & 20 | 5-78 & 2-63 | |
| 8/9/2005 | England | Australia | The Oval | 72 & 8 | 5-78 | |
| 14/10/2005 | World XI | Australia | Sydney | 35 & 15 | 4-59 & 3-48 | |
| 12/11/2005 | England | Pakistan | Multan | 45 & 11 | 4-68 & 4-88 | |
| /11/2005 | England | Pakistan | Faisalabad | 1 & 56 | 1-76 & 3-66 | 2 |
| 29/11/2005 | England | Pakistan | Lahore | 12 & 0 | 1-111 | 1 |
| 1/3/2006 | England | India | Nagpur | 43 | 1-68 & 2-79 | 2 |
| 9/3/2006 | England | India | Mohali | 70 & 51 | 4-96 & 0-11 | 1 |
| 18/3/2006 | England | India | Mumbai | 50 & 50 | 1-68 & 3-14 | |
| 11/5/2006 | England | Sri Lanka | Lord's | 33* | 2-55 & 2-131 | |
| 25/5/2006 | England | Sri Lanka | Birmingham | 9 & 4* | 2-28 & 2-50 | 1 |
| 2/6/2006 | England | Sri Lanka | Nottingham | 1 & 0 | 3-52 & 1-38 | 3 |
| 23/11/2006 | England | Australia | Brisbane | 0 & 16 | 4-99 & 0-11 | |
| 1/12/2006 | England | Australia | Adelaide | 38* & 2 | 1-82 & 2-44 | |
| 14/12/2006 | England | Australia | Perth | 13 & 51 | 0-36 & 0-76 | |
| 26/12/2006 | England | Australia | Melbourne | 13 & 25 | 3-77 | |
| 2/1/2007 | England | Australia | Sydney | 89 & 7 | 1-56 | |
| 18/7/2008 | England | South Africa | Leeds | 17 & 38 | 1-77 | 2 |
| 30/7/2008 | England | South Africa | Birmingham | 36* & 2 | 4-89 & 2-72 | |
| 7/8/2008 | England | South Africa | The Oval | 9 & 11* | 1-37 & 1-53 | 1 |
| 11/12/2008 | England | India | Chennai | 18 & 4 | 3-49 & 1-64 | 2 |
| 19/12/2008 | England | India | Mohali | 62 | 3-54 & 0-39 | |
| 4/2/2009 | England | West Indies | Kingston | 43 & 24 | 2-72 | |
| 13/2/2009 | England | West Indies | North Sound | – | – | |
| 15/2/2009 | England | West Indies | St John's | 0 & 0 | 3-47 & 0-32 | 2 |
| 8/7/2009 | England | Australia | Cardiff | 37 & 26 | 1-128 | |
| 16/7/2009 | England | Australia | Lord's | 4 & 30* | 1-27 & 5-92 | |
| 30/7/2009 | England | Australia | Birmingham | 74 | 0-58 & 0-35 | |
| 20/8/2009 | England | Australia | The Oval | 7 & 22 | 1-35 & 0-42 | 1 |

| TESTS AS CAPTAIN | Opponent | Venue | Toss | Result |
|---|---|---|---|---|
| 1/3/2006 | India | Nagpur | Won | Drawn |
| 9/3/2006 | India | Mohali | Won | Lost |
| 18/3/2006 | India | Mumbai | Lost | Won |
| 11/5/2006 | Sri Lanka | Lord's | Won | Drawn |
| 25/5/2006 | Sri Lanka | Birmingham | Lost | Won |
| 2/6/2006 | Sri Lanka | Nottingham | Lost | Lost |
| 23/11/2006 | Australia | Brisbane | Lost | Lost |
| 1/12/2006 | Australia | Adelaide | Won | Lost |
| 14/12/2006 | Australia | Perth | Lost | Lost |
| 26/12/2006 | Australia | Melbourne | Won | Lost |
| 2/1/2007 | Australia | Sydney | Won | Lost |

| TEST CENTURIES | Team | Opponent | Venue | Season |
|---|---|---|---|---|
| 167 | England | West Indies | Birmingham | 2004 |
| 142 | England | South Africa | Lord's | 2003 |
| 137 | England | New Zealand | Christchurch | 2001–02 |
| 102* | England | West Indies | St John's | 2003–04 |
| 102 | England | Australia | Nottingham | 2005 |

## BREAKDOWN OF TEST BATTING

| | |
|---|---|
| Dots | 4561 |
| Singles | 816 |
| Twos | 190 |
| Threes | 35 |
| Fours | 513 |
| Sixes | 82 |
| **Total Runs** | **3845** |

## RUNS BY BATTING POSITION

| | Inns | NO | Runs | HS | Avge | SR | 100 | 50 |
|---|---|---|---|---|---|---|---|---|
| 4 | 1 | 0 | 75 | 75 | 75.00 | 170.45 | 0 | 1 |
| 5 | 2 | 1 | 61 | 57* | 61.00 | 62.88 | 0 | 1 |
| 6 | 67 | 5 | 1975 | 167 | 31.85 | 57.63 | 3 | 15 |
| 7 | 54 | 3 | 1645 | 142 | 32.25 | 68.05 | 2 | 9 |
| 8 | 5 | 0 | 89 | 38 | 17.80 | 44.05 | 0 | 0 |
| 9 | 1 | 0 | 0 | 0 | 0.00 | 0.00 | 0 | 0 |

**HOW HE WAS DISMISSED**

|  | Times | Total | % |
|---|---|---|---|
| Bowled | 20 | 121 | 16.52 |
| Caught fielder | 61 | 121 | 50.41 |
| Caught keeper | 23 | 121 | 19.00 |
| Lbw | 13 | 121 | 10.74 |
| Other | 0 | 121 | 0.00 |
| Run out | 1 | 121 | 0.82 |
| Stumped | 3 | 121 | 2.47 |

**BOWLERS WHO DISMISSED HIM MORE THAN TWICE**

|  | Times | Matches |
|---|---|---|
| SK Warne | 7 | 11 |
| SM Pollock | 7 | 15 |
| A Kumble | 6 | 8 |
| M Muralitharan | 6 | 8 |
| M Ntini | 5 | 14 |
| JH Kallis | 4 | 17 |
| Shoaib Akhtar | 3 | 3 |
| SR Clark | 3 | 6 |
| PR Adams | 3 | 7 |
| GD McGrath | 3 | 9 |
| B Lee | 3 | 11 |

**BEST BOWLING FIGURES**

|  | Team | Opponent | Venue | Season |
|---|---|---|---|---|
| 5–58 | England | West Indies | Bridgetown | 2003–04 |
| 5–78 | England | Australia | The Oval | 2005 |
| 5–92 | England | Australia | Lord's | 2009 |

**HOW HE TOOK HIS WICKETS**

|  | Times | Total | % |
|---|---|---|---|
| Bowled | 39 | 226 | 17.25 |
| Caught fielder | 103 | 226 | 45.57 |
| Caught keeper | 52 | 226 | 23.00 |
| Hit wicket | 2 | 226 | 0.88 |
| Lbw | 30 | 226 | 13.27 |

## PLAYERS HE DISMISSED MORE THAN TWICE

|  | Times | Matches |
|---|---|---|
| DPMD Jayawardene | 6 | 9 |
| ML Hayden | 6 | 11 |
| ND McKenzie | 5 | 6 |
| SM Katich | 5 | 10 |
| AC Gilchrist | 5 | 11 |
| JL Langer | 5 | 11 |
| SK Warne | 5 | 11 |
| GC Smith | 5 | 13 |
| RT Ponting | 5 | 15 |
| SM Pollock | 5 | 15 |
| JH Kallis | 5 | 17 |
| SP Fleming | 4 | 6 |
| BC Lara | 4 | 9 |
| RR Sarwan | 4 | 11 |
| S Chanderpaul | 4 | 11 |
| Mohammad Yousuf | 3 | 3 |
| TL Best | 3 | 5 |
| W Jaffer | 3 | 5 |
| AJ Hall | 3 | 6 |
| NJ Astle | 3 | 6 |
| DR Martyn | 3 | 7 |
| KC Sangakkara | 3 | 9 |
| VVS Laxman | 3 | 9 |
| B Lee | 3 | 11 |
| RS Dravid | 3 | 11 |
| HH Gibbs | 3 | 13 |
| M Ntini | 3 | 14 |
| MV Boucher | 3 | 16 |

## BATTING PARTNERS

|  | Inns | Unb | Runs | Best | Avge | 100 | 50 |
|---|---|---|---|---|---|---|---|
| GO Jones | 19 | 1 | 1085 | 177 | 60.27 | 5 | 3 |
| GP Thorpe | 20 | 0 | 1082 | 281 | 54.10 | 3 | 4 |
| KP Pietersen | 17 | 0 | 780 | 149 | 45.88 | 2 | 4 |
| PD Collingwood | 19 | 1 | 489 | 84 | 27.16 | 0 | 6 |
| AF Giles | 12 | 1 | 401 | 89 | 36.45 | 0 | 3 |
| N Hussain | 12 | 0 | 291 | 93 | 24.25 | 0 | 2 |
| MJ Prior | 5 | 0 | 241 | 89 | 48.20 | 0 | 3 |
| MP Vaughan | 8 | 1 | 238 | 92 | 34.00 | 0 | 2 |

**BATTING PARTNERS** *(continued)*

| | Inns | Unb | Runs | Best | Avge | 100 | 50 |
|---|---|---|---|---|---|---|---|
| AJ Strauss | 4 | 0 | 200 | 143 | 50.00 | 1 | 0 |
| SJ Harmison | 7 | 0 | 199 | 99 | 28.42 | 0 | 1 |
| MA Butcher | 5 | 0 | 168 | 79 | 33.60 | 0 | 2 |
| AJ Stewart | 9 | 0 | 156 | 97 | 17.33 | 0 | 1 |
| ME Trescothick | 4 | 0 | 127 | 93 | 31.75 | 0 | 1 |
| RWT Key | 1 | 1 | 120 | 120* | – | 1 | 0 |
| GJ Batty | 2 | 0 | 110 | 87 | 55.00 | 0 | 1 |
| MJ Hoggard | 4 | 0 | 109 | 44 | 27.25 | 0 | 0 |
| TR Ambrose | 2 | 0 | 107 | 68 | 53.50 | 0 | 1 |
| AR Caddick | 3 | 0 | 107 | 55 | 35.66 | 0 | 2 |
| IR Bell | 9 | 0 | 106 | 27 | 11.77 | 0 | 0 |
| SP Jones | 3 | 1 | 101 | 51 | 50.50 | 0 | 1 |
| SCJ Broad | 5 | 1 | 100 | 52 | 25.00 | 0 | 1 |
| CMW Read | 5 | 0 | 100 | 59 | 20.00 | 0 | 1 |
| JM Anderson | 6 | 0 | 76 | 46 | 12.66 | 0 | 0 |
| D Gough | 3 | 0 | 72 | 47 | 24.00 | 0 | 0 |
| JH Kallis | 2 | 0 | 64 | 52 | 32.00 | 0 | 1 |
| MR Ramprakash | 4 | 0 | 59 | 31 | 14.75 | 0 | 0 |
| IJL Trott | 2 | 0 | 50 | 32 | 25.00 | 0 | 0 |
| NV Knight | 2 | 0 | 48 | 30 | 24.00 | 0 | 0 |
| MA Atherton | 1 | 0 | 43 | 43 | 43.00 | 0 | 0 |
| MP Bicknell | 3 | 0 | 41 | 28 | 13.66 | 0 | 0 |
| JP Crawley | 2 | 0 | 38 | 23 | 19.00 | 0 | 0 |
| DL Vettori | 1 | 0 | 32 | 32 | 32.00 | 0 | 0 |
| CJ Adams | 2 | 0 | 30 | 17 | 15.00 | 0 | 0 |
| GA Hick | 2 | 0 | 29 | 29 | 14.50 | 0 | 0 |
| RJ Kirtley | 2 | 0 | 27 | 14 | 13.50 | 0 | 0 |
| RJ Sidebottom | 2 | 0 | 27 | 24 | 13.50 | 0 | 0 |
| MS Panesar | 3 | 0 | 10 | 9 | 3.33 | 0 | 0 |
| AN Cook | 1 | 1 | 8 | 8* | – | 0 | 0 |
| LE Plunkett | 1 | 0 | 8 | 8 | 8.00 | 0 | 0 |
| MV Boucher | 1 | 0 | 4 | 4 | 4.00 | 0 | 0 |
| Kabir Ali | 1 | 0 | 4 | 4 | 4.00 | 0 | 0 |
| C White | 1 | 0 | 3 | 3 | 3.00 | 0 | 0 |
| JS Foster | 1 | 0 | 2 | 2 | 2.00 | 0 | 0 |
| OA Shah | 1 | 0 | 2 | 2 | 2.00 | 0 | 0 |
| GM Hamilton | 2 | 0 | 1 | 1 | 0.50 | 0 | 0 |
| RDB Croft | 1 | 0 | 0 | 0 | 0.00 | 0 | 0 |
| A McGrath | 1 | 0 | 0 | 0 | 0.00 | 0 | 0 |
| SI Mahmood | 1 | 0 | 0 | 0 | 0.00 | 0 | 0 |